Reimagining Student Engagement

Reimagining Student Engagement

From Disrupting to Driving

Amy Berry

Foreword by John Hattie

A SAGE Publishing Company

FOR INFORMATION:

Corwin
A SAGE Company
2455 Teller Road
Thousand Oaks, California 91320
(800) 233-9936
www.corwin.com

SAGE Publications Ltd.
1 Oliver's Yard
55 City Road
London EC1Y 1SP
United Kingdom

SAGE Publications India Pvt. Ltd.
B 1/I 1 Mohan Cooperative Industrial Area
Mathura Road, New Delhi 110 044
India

SAGE Publications Asia-Pacific Pte. Ltd.
18 Cross Street #10-10/11/12
China Square Central
Singapore 048423

President: Mike Soules
Vice President and Editorial Director: Monica Eckman
Publisher: Jessica Allan
Senior Content Development Editor: Lucas Schleicher
Associate Content Development Editor: Mia Rodriguez
Editorial Assistant: Natalie Delpino
Production Editor: Tori Mirsadjadi
Copy Editor: Melinda Masson
Typesetter: Exeter Premedia Services
Proofreader: Barbara Coster
Cover Designer: Gail Buschman
Marketing Manager: Olivia Bartlett

Contents

Foreword

Every night, teachers ponder how to find, adapt, or devise activities to engage their students in the next day's learning. Thus, it is no surprise that engagement is a major topic of interest, research, and discussion. When you ask teachers how they know their students are learning, they often answer in terms of their engagement with the lesson: They are doing the work, completing it, and handing it in. For some teachers, being *engaged* is akin to how we use the term before marriage—a formal arrangement to do something. For some students, being engaged in lessons is akin to how the armed forces use the word *engagement*—a battle to be fought.

It seems ironic that there is so little evidence of the engagement power of lessons. Indeed, there is little evidence of the impact of lesson plans. Further, students engaged or "doing the work" correlates with but is not necessarily learning. In a lot of "doing" there may be little learning. Students can be turned off to learning, become bored or disruptive, or withdraw when asked to just "do" work that has little relevance or meaning.

There is, however, a rich literature that is usually based on the notion of behavioral, cognitive, and emotional engagement. There are measures resplendent with factor analyses, structural models, and high alphas. Seductive indeed. But they predict so little. A new broom is sorely needed.

A few years back, a new student enrolled at the University of Melbourne to complete a PhD, which in the Australian system is a three- to four-year journey solely conducting a research study (or studies). Think of this model. Amy Berry, the student, pays to complete a four-year degree, delves deeply into a topic, designs and runs a series of studies, conducts the analyses, and writes her thesis. In this process, she allows me (her supervisor) to be a critic, listener, and prompter and to ensure that the project has big ideas that can make a contribution. She does the hard work, and I become the learner and thus a major beneficiary of this process. And I get paid to do this. Amy is number 204 of my thesis students, and this book is a testament to a dedicated, diligent, and driven student who discovered a "big idea" that is the focus of this book.

The work did not stop upon graduation but continued in Amy's subsequent roles. This book is the outcome of a sustained, deeply thoughtful, practical, and scientific process. It started in the field asking teachers about their concept of engagement, moved to the development and testing of a model, and morphed into experimenting with practical strategies to move students along the engagement continuum.

Engagement is not a "thing" but a process of moving from disrupting, avoiding, and withdrawing to participating, investing, and driving. It assumes students have rich and deep motivating resources, but the art is to have them invest these resources in valuable classwork rather than saving the resources for sports, social life, or media engagement. It involves, like an engagement to be married, a commitment, a pact, and a promise—that learning will occur, that there will be fun and hard work along the way, and that students and teachers can engage in the love of learning. It will entail battles, discovering that failure is a learner's best friend and that struggling is desirable, and involves moving from participating through investing to driving. This book will change many ideas about the meaning of engagement and open many eyes to the exciting possibilities of engaging students in learning.

John Hattie

Acknowledgments

This book would not have been possible without the generous support of John Hattie. His guidance and encouragement during my research led to the continuum of engagement upon which this book is based. His belief in the continuum has meant that instead of being confined to the pages of a journal article, it continues to find its way into classrooms and into the hands of teachers and students. John has gone above and beyond in writing the foreword for the book and providing invaluable feedback and advice on the draft, for which I am very grateful.

I would also like to express my sincere thanks to Doug Fisher and Nancy Frey for their continued support. When John, Doug, and Nancy decided to include the continuum in *The Distance Learning Playbook*, I was excited but had no way of knowing that this would be the catalyst that finally had me writing the book on student engagement that I had long been contemplating. Like John, Doug and Nancy have been active supporters of the continuum and continue to share the success stories of how teachers and students are using it to improve engagement and learning in schools. To all of the teachers, parents, and students who have shared their experiences and insights, you have provided powerful motivation to write this book and take the ideas further.

Finally, I would like to thank my friends and family who have shown continued interest in the book and celebrated each milestone with me. To my husband, Craig, thank you for being my biggest supporter and most passionate cheerleader.

About the Author

Dr. Amy Berry is a research fellow at the Australian Council for Educational Research and an honorary fellow at the University of Melbourne. Amy began her career as a primary school teacher in Queensland before returning to university to complete a master of education (research). Having developed a passion for research, she went on to complete her PhD looking at teacher perspectives on student engagement and their approaches to engaging students in classroom learning. Amy has extensive experience working with preservice and practicing teachers to develop their skills in classroom-based assessment and evidence-based practice. She has designed numerous professional learning programs for teachers, including programs on formative assessment, student engagement, and learning through play. As well as working with teachers in Australia, Amy has worked with teachers, school leaders, and education officials from Saudi Arabia, Singapore, Indonesia, the Philippines, and Ukraine.

Introduction

· ·

WHY ENGAGEMENT?

"There is a yawning gap between the ways in which schools are organized and what we know promotes positive youth development and learning. . . . [T]here is a critical need to examine efforts to change the grammar of schooling, given the misalignment between this grammar and much of what we know would provide thriving conditions for youth."

—Jal Mehta and Amanda Datnow (2020, p. 492)

Before becoming a primary school teacher, I was in charge of the *Responsible Thinking Classroom* at a local high school. The idea was that teachers would use a series of prompts to encourage disruptive students to make a more "responsible" choice, and if they did not comply, they came to me. While not the intention, it was seen by many as the naughty kids' room. Some students came in angry and raging at the injustice of it all, and "They've got it in for me!" was a frequent complaint. At times, their frustration was so great they were reduced to tears. Other students were happy to escape their classroom and strolled in with satisfied smiles and a wave as they walked to a seat to fill out the required paperwork. I would meet with each one as they came in, hear their side of the story, and help them fill out their form. The final step in the process was to facilitate a meeting between the teacher and the student. The student would explain their view of the events and their plans for preventing similar events in the future, often followed by an earful from the teacher about making better choices. Then the green light was given for the student to rejoin the class in the next lesson. It was not designed to be punitive or controlling, but there was no denying that this had become a ritualized battle over compliance. In some cases, a student would only come through my room once or twice—perhaps just having a bad day. However, there were also frequent flyers who I saw every week or even every day.

Later, I moved into a part-time role in the same school providing support for individual students who were failing to meet the expected outcomes for learning. It may have been a different room and a different context, but many of the faces and names were all too familiar to me. It was clear that these students had a very different experience of school than I had growing up. For these students, school was not about learning, improving, and achieving success. Instead, school was a daily battle and a daily reminder of their failings.

These experiences stuck with me over the years. At the time, it motivated me to return to university, filled with optimism and a desire to create a better experience of learning and school for all those "naughty kids" out there. I still feel that same deep desire for change, but I see now that the problem is much bigger than I once thought. Disengagement takes many forms and affects students across all levels of achievement, socioeconomic backgrounds, and ages. Disruptive students who actively demonstrate their disengagement and disenchantment with school are the most visible, but they are merely the tip of the iceberg. Less visible, but no less concerning, is the large number of students who are passively disengaged and disconnected from learning at school. They choose this path for a number of different reasons, but the result is the same. They fly under the radar on a pathway that limits both their potential for learning and their ability to thrive at school. Student engagement has been frequently linked to desirable outcomes such as achievement, academic success, and student well-being, making it a valued goal for the education community. The quest to improve student engagement in our schools has attracted the attention of researchers, policymakers, and practitioners for well over two decades. Despite this attention, it remains that schools and teachers continue to struggle with the persistent challenge of improving student engagement in learning—a challenge that was only heightened by the educational disruptions of COVID-19.

Although the push to reform education is constant, the traditional practices, rules, and structures that characterize what happens in schools—often referred to as the "grammar of schooling" (Tyack & Tobin, 1994)—have proven to be stubbornly impervious to change. As David Labaree (2021) noted, "Innovative reform efforts bombard schools constantly, but they nearly always seem to bounce off the classroom door, having little to no effect on how teachers teach and students learn" (p. 28). This includes efforts to improve student engagement, with the entrenched norms presenting a significant roadblock to change. Within the traditional grammar of schooling, the implicit expectation is that students will be passive recipients of instruction and compliant participants in learning activities. Teachers are responsible for delivering instruction, giving students something to do, and monitoring student compliance and achievement. As alluded to in the opening quote, this runs counter to what we know about promoting student learning and well-being (Mehta & Datnow, 2020) and what we know about motivation and engagement. To thrive, students need to feel connected to their peers and the teacher, feel valued and appreciated within the classroom community, and be given a voice in learning. They need to be involved in work that is meaningful, relates to their lives, and has a clear purpose. They need to be actively involved in learning, motivated to learn, and able to connect with their peers during learning. Instead, the existing grammar of schooling sets the scene for passivity, frustration, boredom, apathy, and an ongoing battle over compliance. With the bedrock of this grammar of schooling firmly in place, it is little wonder that despite decades of attention at the research and policy levels, we appear no closer to achieving the goal of greater student engagement in our classrooms.

Rather than tinkering around the edges of the existing grammar of schooling, a more substantial reimagining of student engagement is needed—one that challenges the existing conceptions of passive students who need to be pushed or pulled by the teacher to get motivated and engaged, and teachers as the drivers of learning and engagement. The view of engagement that you will read about in this book positions students as active and agentic partners in engagement who possess rich inner motivational resources that provide valuable fuel for engagement and learning, should the student choose to invest them. It views students as competent partners who are capable of developing the skills and knowledge that will enable them to regulate their engagement and actively drive their learning forward. Teachers share the responsibility for engagement with students, and their role is no less important. They provide the necessary support, structure, and opportunities for students to become actively engaged, autonomous, and successful learners. Teachers are valued not just for their pedagogical expertise and managerial capabilities, but also for their ability to become actively engaged in the engagement process with their students.

This book has three main aims: developing a richer vocabulary for engagement that is accessible and meaningful to teachers *and* students, redefining the roles and rules of engagement, and describing a process for engagement embedded in the learning experience. Along the way, you will be invited to reflect on your own experiences of teaching and learning, hear from others about their experiences of student engagement, and think about the pathway and steps that you will take with your students as you reimagine engagement in your classroom.

CHAPTER 1

What Do We Mean by Engagement? The Illusion of Consensus

"Of course we want our students to be engaged. Doesn't everyone want that? I mean, that's just a given."

I f you've spent any time in and around schools, you may be so familiar with the term *engagement* that you don't even notice how often people use it during everyday conversations about teaching and learning. It has become a part of our school vernacular to the point that it is assumed everyone knows what it means. One of my colleagues once cornered me in the hallway to exclaim, "Ever since your presentation last week, all I hear about is engagement. I can't believe how much people use that word! It's driving me nuts!"

One of the challenges of student engagement lies in the term's familiarity and the frequency with which it is used. In 2016, Jacquelynne Eccles warned, "[T]he popularity and seeming familiarity of engagement as a concept" brings with it "the danger that, although we believe we are communicating well, we are actually talking about very different things" (pp. 72–73). While all of us have experience using the term, how often have you been asked to explain what you mean? Understanding what is meant by *student engagement* has become a form of assumed knowledge for anyone working in schools these days. Not only do we assume everyone understands the concept, but we also assume there is a level of consensus about that meaning among those in the education community. As we will soon see, this is not true. Before we turn our attention to frameworks for describing engagement, take a moment to reflect on your own understanding of the concept.

TIME TO REFLECT

If you were asked to describe what student engagement means to you, what would you say? What does student engagement look like or sound like in your classroom? How do you detect whether students are engaged or not? Make some notes to record your thoughts; we will return to them at the end of this chapter.

Now draw a line underneath your notes and consider the next question. Can you think of a time when your students were especially engaged in something they were doing in class? What was happening that told you they were really engaged in this? What did it look like or sound like? Add these notes under the line.

Ask five of your colleagues to explain what they mean by engagement. How do they know when their students are engaged?

ENGAGEMENT AS A PSYCHOLOGICAL CONCEPT

One of the most common ways of describing engagement comes from the field of educational psychology and research into human motivation. The predominant framework for engagement was proposed by Jennifer Fredricks, Phyllis Blumenfeld, and Alison Paris in 2004. They characterized engagement as having three dimensions: a behavioral dimension, a cognitive dimension, and an emotional dimension.

- **Behavioral engagement** describes behaviors such as following rules, attendance at school, paying attention, showing concentration, contributing to class discussions, being on task, and participating in school activities.

- **Emotional engagement** refers to students' attitudes toward school and toward learning, as well as their feelings about school and learning. These feelings include things like belonging, happiness, sadness, anxiety, interest, and valuing success in school.

- **Cognitive engagement** relates to students' psychological investment in learning and their use of strategies for learning. This includes things like going beyond what is required in a task, seeking out challenges, demonstrating a resilience to failure, and having a desire to master the knowledge and skills that are taught. There is also a significant overlap between the concept of self-regulated learning and the use of metacognitive strategies in pursuit of a learning goal.

This is not to suggest that everyone agrees on this description of engagement. Other dimensions have been proposed, including academic engagement, social engagement, collaborative engagement, and agentic engagement. Even when researchers agree on the dimensions, they don't always agree with each other on how to categorize things under those dimensions. For example, some label "effort" as an example of behavioral engagement, while others see it as an example of cognitive engagement.

This model has generated many measures and models, and it is seductive and clear—but how useful is it to enhance engagement in your students, and do the three components predict much? Despite its popularity in education policy, questions remain about how useful this framework is to teachers and how well it represents their daily experiences of student engagement.

WHAT DO YOU THINK?

Now that you've read about the three-dimensional framework for describing engagement, have a look back at the notes you made when reflecting on what student engagement looks like and sounds like in your classroom. Can you see things that might be categorized as behavioral engagement? Emotional engagement? Cognitive engagement?

Are there things on your list that don't seem to fit in those categories?

(Continued)

(Continued)

Can you fit the five teachers' comments about their notions of engagement into one of these three dimensions?

ENGAGEMENT AS A SCHOOL PROBLEM

It is difficult to discuss the concept of engagement without also thinking about what it means to be disengaged. In my own research, many teachers often referenced disengagement as a way of explaining engagement. You can see this in the following comment:

> *"They are just so engaged and so enthusiastic about learning.*
> *You can see it in their independence and just the effort*
> *they put in. Because there are others who are the opposite,*
> *who are never engaged. There's a couple that just go,*
> *'Yeah, school's boring.'"*

Along with being described as a psychological concept, student engagement is often viewed through a deficit lens that focuses on disengagement. This perspective is primarily interested in systemic issues such as preventing school dropout and the negative impact of disengaged students on teachers and classrooms. As a result, work in this area concentrates on students identified as either disengaged or at risk of disengaging from school, rather than how teachers promote the engagement of all students in daily learning experiences in the classroom.

Many researchers have reported a pattern of decreasing engagement as students move through school, particularly in the transition from elementary to high school. Others have described concerning rates of disengagement within schools and the negative consequences for both students and teachers. A recent report into student engagement in Australian schools described widespread disengagement with roughly 40 percent of students regularly disengaged in the classroom, over half of whom were categorized as compliant but "quietly disengaged" (Goss et al., 2017, p. 10). In the United States, it has been reported that only 47 percent of students are engaged in school (Hodges, 2018), and around half of the students surveyed by the Association for Supervision and Curriculum Development (ASCD, 2016) said they were bored every day at school.

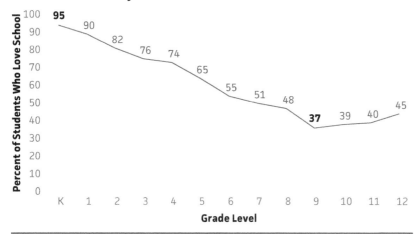

FIGURE 1.1 ● The Jenkins Curve

Source: Jenkins, n.d.

Anyone who has listened to John Hattie speak might be familiar with the Jenkins Curve research. Lee Jenkins (n.d.) surveyed three thousand teachers and asked them two questions: *What grade level do you teach? What percentage of students at this grade level love school?* The results, presented in Figure 1.1, show a dramatic decline in enthusiasm for school as students move through the system. Teachers reported that 95 percent of kindergarten students loved school, but that level dropped to 37 percent for Grade 9 students. Despite believing that students only started to lose their enthusiasm for school once they transitioned out of elementary school, Jenkins found that loss of love for school actually begins in kindergarten and Grade 1. It is true that "love of school" does not necessarily mean "love of learning at school," as some students love school for the social aspects or extra-curricular activities like sports or music. It's fair to assume that if we asked specifically about loving learning at school, the numbers would be even worse than those shown in the Jenkins Curve.

Teacher experience is no remedy for student engagement, with experienced teachers experiencing the same rates of disengagement as those new to the profession. Student disengagement can take its toll on teachers, potentially leading to decreased well-being and burnout. However, we also have compelling evidence to suggest that schools and teachers have the ability to effectively intervene and positively influence students' engagement in school and in learning even when there are factors that are predictive of disengagement and dropout (e.g., low socioeconomic status).

engagement (n)

1600s, "formal promise," from French *engagement* and Old French *engagier*, meaning "make a pledge." Also indicates a hostile encounter or battle between armed forces.

1700s, a formal agreement to get married.

Apparently being engaged means we are either going to war with each other or getting married! As strange as it may sound on the surface, this could actually be closer to the mark than you might think.

Who gets to decide whether a student is pronounced "engaged" or "disengaged"? Generally speaking, it is the adults who make the rules for engagement, and students are expected to follow them. Many teachers and schools continue to blame students for their disengagement, rather than reflecting on how the environment influences engagement. In this situation, the disengaged student becomes the opponent who fails to play by the rules. In the context of classroom learning, the teacher makes plans for teaching and learning, and these plans include expectations for how students will engage in the planned activities. It is the teacher's plans for the learning experience that serve as the reference point for engagement. Are students engaged in the teacher's plans for learning, or are they disengaged from those plans? Battle lines are drawn.

Importantly, the fact that individual students are doing an activity the teacher has planned for them does not necessarily mean there aren't other things they would rather be learning or engaged in doing. Similarly, students may be disengaged from the planned learning activity but actively engaged in something else. Just as students are not empty vessels waiting to be filled with knowledge, they are not devoid of their own rich motivational resources. They bring to the classroom a range of motivational resources that can be fuel for engagement—such as personal interests, relationships with peers, curiosity, and previous experiences of success. The question is not whether students are motivated or not motivated. The question is whether they are motivated to learn what we want them to learn and do what we want them to do. It is a matter not of switching on motivation, but of directing their motivation to worthwhile challenging learning. Students have a choice to make when it comes to where they will invest their motivation and to what degree they will invest. These choices have implications for their engagement in classroom learning experiences. Our challenge as teachers is not to push or pull students in the direction we want them to go, but to work in partnership with them to create opportunities for learning that they want to invest their motivational resources in pursuing.

Before we move on, let's take a moment to reflect on our experiences with student disengagement.

TIME TO REFLECT

If you were asked to describe what student disengagement means to you, what would you say? What does disengagement look like or sound like in your classroom? Add these to your notes about engagement.

ENGAGEMENT IN WHAT?

Engagement must have a context. We engage *in* something or *with* something, or we disengage *from* something. Research into student engagement looks at many different contexts for engagement ranging from engaging in the social institution that is "school" to engaging in the process of learning something. To better understand the value of engagement and its role in supporting specific outcomes, it is useful to look at the different lines of engagement research.

WHAT DOES THE RESEARCH SAY?

Broadly speaking, student engagement in school has been repeatedly associated with achievement and academic success, and a lack of engagement in school has been associated with less desirable outcomes such as school dropout. Engagement has the potential to help students persist with challenging tasks, remain resilient in the face of setbacks or failures in learning and at school, and experience greater well-being.

Many schools and districts collect data on student disengagement to identify at-risk students. These data tend to rely on things relating to students' behavior at school, like attendance and suspensions, rather than things relating to students' emotional or cognitive engagement in learning. Disengagement tends to be higher in urban schools and among males, students from minority groups, and students from lower socioeconomic households (Fredricks et al., 2019).

While there is a general pattern of declining engagement as students progress through school, distinct engagement patterns have been identified by researchers. Some students have fairly stable patterns of engagement (sometimes consistently low), and others have a more rapid drop in engagement over time (Janosz et al., 2008). Students can show different patterns of engagement that suggest being successful at school does not necessarily equate to being fully invested in learning. That is, students can be achieving and going through the motions of "doing school" but also report feeling bored, feeling stressed, and not learning anything (Conner & Pope, 2013; Pope, 2001; Wang & Peck, 2013).

One way to think about this is to make a distinction between "engaging in school" and "engaging in learning." When we are thinking about students engaging in school, we are interested in things like attendance, involvement in the activities that happen at school, and adherence to the rules and social norms of the school. While these things may contribute to preventing dropout and supporting a sense of belonging within the school community, it is unlikely that these aspects of engagement will be sufficient in promoting learning.

As teachers, we want our students to feel invested and involved in school, but we are also interested in how students engage in learning. This might include involvement in planned learning experiences, willingness to take on challenges, collaborating with peers, and applying a range of cognitive and metacognitive strategies to support their learning. The focus of this book will be on fostering student engagement in learning in a way that will also support their needs for autonomy and competence as learners and their feelings of being meaningfully connected to others in learning.

ENGAGEMENT FOR WHAT PURPOSE?

Being clear on what students will be engaged in is only one side of the coin. On the flip side, we need to consider why we are interested in their engagement and what purpose it will serve. Engagement has been associated with a number of different outcomes that might be of interest to schools and teachers. These include achievement and academic success, as well as feelings of well-being and connection to others at school. In order for us to choose strategies for facilitating student engagement, we need to think about the outcomes we are hoping to influence and how success will be measured. Let's consider the following scenarios:

Scenario 1

Paul wants to improve student well-being in his class. In particular, he is interested in fostering a greater sense of social connection within the class and positive feelings about being at school and in this class. He has selected a number of strategies that he hopes might improve their engagement in an upcoming unit of work. These include opportunities to work in teams, giving them some choice in what they will do in that team, and using an open-ended task. He is hoping to evaluate the effectiveness of these strategies by looking at their completed tasks.

Scenario 2

Tanya wants to improve her students' skills in researching historical events and deepen their knowledge of a key historical event. She is hoping that including a number of engaging elements, such as videos and a game related to this historical event, might help students to be more engaged in their learning. In her planning, she has developed a short feedback form to get students to rate their enjoyment of the different activities.

Both teachers are interested in increasing the engagement of their students, but for very different reasons. Paul is hoping engagement will positively influence student attitudes and feelings about school, while Tanya is hoping engagement will lead to improvements in understanding and specific skills. Looking at their plans for evaluating their impact, do you think the teachers will have the evidence they need to determine if their engagement strategies "worked"?

Ideally, we are hoping to align our intentions for engagement, and the strategies we will use to facilitate engagement, with our intended outcomes. In addition, we want to align our strategies for collecting evidence and evaluating our impact with the intentions for engagement and the intended outcomes. In order to do this, we need to be explicit about what the students will engage in and what intended outcome this engagement is intended to support.

ENGAGEMENT FROM THE TEACHER'S PERSPECTIVE

Despite an abundance of research into student engagement and evidence to show the influence teachers have on the engagement of their students, very few have investigated how teachers think about engagement. Do teachers make distinctions between emotional engagement, behavioral engagement, and cognitive engagement? Do they focus on disengagement and fixing problems with engagement? Or, do they have other ways of thinking about student engagement?

My work as a classroom teacher inspired these questions and others and formed the basis for my research into teacher perspectives on engagement. Rather than contesting the existing approaches to engagement, this work sought to add an additional vantage point for thinking about and discussing student engagement, one that is embedded in the daily life of the classroom.

As teachers, the way we conceptualize student engagement is the result of many things. One of the primary influences on our understanding of engagement is our prior experiences in the classroom. This may relate to both our experiences as students and our experiences as teachers attempting to engage students within lessons. In my research, many of the teachers' descriptions of the concept of engagement involved recounting specific episodes in the classroom either as a way of illustrating what they were trying to convey or as a way of thinking through and reflecting on what they knew of engagement. You may have found yourself doing this same thing when you reflected on what engagement and disengagement mean to you. A key finding from my research was that teachers have a range of meanings when they use the broad terms *engagement* and *disengagement*. Not only do different teachers describe engagement in different ways, but individual teachers also express a range of different meanings for the concept of engagement.

So much for the illusion of consensus. So much for immaculate perception.

DISRUPTING TO DRIVING: A CONTINUUM OF STUDENT ENGAGEMENT

In 2016–2017, I decided to investigate the concept of student engagement from the perspective of the classroom teacher. I conducted in-depth interviews with teachers to explore their conceptions of student engagement in learning. The reflection prompts that you've used in this chapter are similar to some of the questions I asked these teachers. In particular, I was interested in both the everyday examples of student engagement these teachers described, as well as their descriptions of less common, but often powerful, examples of highly engaged students. In this way, I was trying to capture the full range of engagement that teachers might encounter in the classroom. Since this research, I have had many other opportunities to ask teachers to describe engagement and recount their experiences of student engagement in the classroom. I've also received feedback from teachers, parents, and others in the education community to suggest that the forms of engagement I described resonate with their own experiences and provide a useful reference point for their work with students. In 2020, Douglas Fisher, Nancy Frey, and John Hattie included the continuum in *The Distance Learning Playbook*, introducing it to a wide range of education professionals and extending it beyond its origins in the classroom and into the realm of distance learning.

Using teachers' descriptions of engagement from the interviews, I created a continuum describing six different forms of engagement in the planned learning experience (Berry, 2020). This includes their engagement *in* the activity, as well as their engagement *with* peers during the planned activity. In Figure 1.2, on the left are three forms of students disengaging from the planned learning experience, and on the right are three forms of students engaging in the learning experience. The most active forms are on either end, and the most passive forms are in the middle. Finally, possible goals that a teacher might have for student engagement in the learning experience are offered as a way of connecting teacher expectations with the different forms of engagement.

Let's take a closer look at these six forms of engagement, beginning with three ways that students engage in the planned learning experience. These forms range from passively participating and going along with what the teacher has planned, to actively investing in the focus for learning and driving their progress toward meaningful goals for learning.

FIGURE 1.2 ● *Disrupting* to *Driving*: A Continuum of Student Engagement

ACTIVE ←——— PASSIVE ———→ ACTIVE

	DISRUPTING	AVOIDING	WITHDRAWING	PARTICIPATING	INVESTING	DRIVING
Engaging in the activity	Disrupting the learning environment Refusing to participate Arguing with the teacher	Looking for ways to avoid work Being off-task Being unprepared Looking for reasons to leave the room or move around the room	"Flying under the radar" Physically separating from others Being distracted Putting in low effort	Doing the work Being on task Paying attention Responding to questions	Asking questions about what we are learning Valuing what we are learning Showing interest or curiosity in what we are learning Enjoying learning	Setting goals for my learning Seeking feedback to help me improve Seeking out challenges Monitoring and evaluating my progress
Engaging with peers	Arguing with peers Trying to distract others	Off-task talking with others Playing around with others instead of working	Sitting with a group if directed but not interacting	Working with others when directed to do so	Sharing ideas and thinking with peers Following shared interests	Collaborating with others toward a shared goal Challenging each other to drive improvement
	Students are **disengaging** from the planned learning experience			Students are **engaging** in the planned learning experience		
What goals might the teacher have for engagement in the learning experience?				I want them to follow my lead and complete certain tasks	I want them to be interested in learning and actively involved in the process	I want them to be proactive and collaborative learners

PARTICIPATING

"Probably the first thing is where their focus is at, so if they're looking at their work or quietly completing the task."

This form of engagement is characterized by students' compliant behavior and willingness to do what the teacher has asked them to do. Behaviors associated with this type of engagement include being on task, being focused, paying attention, doing work, and responding to teacher questions. In relation to engaging with peers, this is limited to working in groups or pairs when directed to do so by the teacher. When expectations for engagement sit at this level, the focus is on listening to the teacher, following the teacher's instructions, and completing the tasks that have been assigned by the teacher.

INVESTING

"Students who are engaged ask a lot of questions, are keen and curious, want to know more, and think actively about what they are working on."

When students move from passive compliance to this more active form of engagement, we see signs that they are personally invested in and finding value in what they are learning. Behaviors include showing curiosity and interest, displaying signs they are enjoying learning, asking questions about what they are learning, engaging in discussions about the learning, and thinking more deeply about what they are learning. This includes wanting to share their questions, ideas, and experiences with peers during the learning experience, either as part of a whole-class discussion or during small-group activities. When expectations for engagement sit at this level, the focus is on deeper thinking, more active involvement in learning, and students feeling that what they are learning is both interesting and meaningful.

DRIVING

"That was important to them. That was the focus that was driving them, and every thought they had was what they wanted to do. They kept asking, 'When are we having time to plan?'"

In this most active form of engagement, students are striving toward a goal they have set for themselves, one that is personally meaningful to them and involves a certain level of challenge. We sometimes refer to this kind of challenge as "hard fun." Behaviors associated with *driving* include setting goals for learning; engaging in self-reflection, self-assessment, and self-evaluation; seeking feedback to help them improve; and looking for ways to extend their learning. At this level, engagement with peers is also at its highest level. This can include actively collaborating with others to learn together and actively seeking out peers as a valuable source of feedback and support during learning. When expectations for engagement are at this level, the focus is on wanting students to successfully "drive" their own learning, either individually or collaboratively, and make use of available resources (including peers) to support improvements in learning.

When students are *driving*, they are becoming masters of their own learning and engaging in behaviors characteristic of *self-regulated learning*. This includes setting goals for improving, making a plan for improvement, taking actions and using strategies to achieve that goal, monitoring and evaluating progress toward the goal, and using feedback to guide improvement (Panadero, 2017).

Three forms describe students disengaging from the planned learning activity; they range from passive withdrawal through actively attempting to disrupt the learning environment.

WITHDRAWING

"They've just pulled the blinds down; you can see them automatically glaze over, and it doesn't matter what you're saying—you've lost them."

Students who are passively disengaged in the learning experience are often described as "flying under the radar." They are not trying to call attention to themselves or cause any disruption, but they are also not participating in the planned learning experience. Behaviors that are associated with this form of disengagement include appearing distracted, not making eye contact, daydreaming, physically withdrawing from the group, staring out the window, and lacking participation or effort. In this passive form of disengaging from the learning experience, students are only engaging with peers when directed to do so by the teacher. This may involve sitting with a group as part of a group activity but not interacting with others during the activity.

Some students actively engage in not being visible to the teacher, hoping never to be asked questions in class, and seeming like they are there but not. While this may seem like a harmless form of disengaging, the impact of passive disengagement on learning is just as serious as the more active forms of disengaging (Angus et al., 2009).

AVOIDING

"They find excuses to go out of the room a lot, or go to their bag a lot. They sit on the computer and find other things to do instead of staying on task."

Students at this level of disengagement are often described as being off task and actively looking to avoid engaging in the planned learning experience. Unlike the *withdrawing* form, students are not as concerned with going unnoticed, and they are actively seeking out other things to do rather than passively disengaging. Behaviors associated with this form of disengagement include moving around the room unnecessarily, being off task, asking to leave the room, and being unprepared. In relation to engaging with peers, students may engage in off-task behavior like talking or playing with materials with other students who are also looking to avoid engaging in the planned learning activity.

DISRUPTING

"They go around to someone else's desk and start an argument about something—goofing around, being loud, and causing a bit of trouble."

In this form of disengagement, students are actively disrupting the learning environment or explicitly refusing to participate in the planned learning experience. Behaviors include arguing with the teacher or peers, being noncompliant, trying to distract others, and moving around the room in a way that causes a disruption to learning (e.g., running around, rolling around on chairs). In relation to engaging with peers, students at this level might get into arguments with peers or try to distract them by attempting to attract their attention away from the planned learning activity. They can be actively engaged in being disruptive, and reprimands can reinforce these behaviors by showing the disruptive students and their peers how successful they can be in their disrupting role.

This continuum offers an additional vantage point from which we can think about student engagement, this time from the perspective of the teacher, and an expanded vocabulary for discussing engagement within the context of classroom learning. In the coming chapters, we will continue to explore how this continuum might be used in planning for, reflecting on, and evaluating student engagement in learning. First, take a moment to return to your notes and reflect on them through the lens of the continuum.

TIME TO REFLECT

Looking back at your notes on engagement and disengagement, can you see some connection to the different forms described in the continuum? What forms can you see represented in your notes? Are there any forms that are absent in your notes?

Can you think of examples of each of the forms of engagement and disengagement from your own experiences in the classroom?

CHAPTER 2

Engagement as a Partnership

"It's difficult. At the start, I thought, 'Right, I'm going to take you in this direction. It's going to be great, and you're going to achieve these standards that the principal is wanting.' And now I'm finding, oh no, we're not quite going to get there like I thought we were. I thought they'd get on board, and they'd be excited, and they'd be achieving, and then we'd build . . . but they're not wanting to put the work in or the effort in. They don't get as excited by success as I thought they might. It's a constant battle to try and engage them."

—Teacher in her first year at a new school

In the previous chapter, we saw that engagement can be viewed as a battlefield, pitting teachers who have set the rules of engagement against students who choose not to play by those rules. While the balance of power is undeniably in favor of the teacher when it comes to planning what the students will be expected to do in a lesson, it is up to the students themselves to decide whether or not they will come to the party—and to what degree they will join the party or try and break it up. As we see in the opening quote, our engagement and motivation as teachers can become collateral damage when we feel caught in the middle of pressure from above and resistance from below.

Mary Kennedy (2016) identified student engagement as one of five persistent and pervasive problems of practice faced by teachers. This problem stems from the fact that while we may be able to force students to turn up to school, we can't force them to learn once they are there. Students have three choices available to them in the face of this "forced captivity"—active engagement, active resistance, or passive compliance. Kennedy went on to argue that the challenge of trying to get all students actively engaged in every lesson is so great that teachers might opt to settle for a more realistic goal of passive compliance.

A truce, as it were, with no clear winners in terms of either engagement or learning.

Students walk into classes with enormous reserves of motivation—their interests, passions, capacity for curiosity, and natural inclination to connect with others, to name a few—but many do not want to spend these resources on school learning. Our role, as teachers, is to turn these resources into fuel for learning so that students want to invest effort and energy into their work at school, and enjoy the success that comes from that effort. This is a major point of engagement. It is less about pushing and pulling them in the direction we want them to go, and more about making learning the pathway they want to be on. It is steering these rich resources to the tasks most likely to have them investing and driving toward success in lessons.

AN ALTERNATIVE MODEL: ENGAGEMENT AS A PARTNERSHIP

"In many schools, students feel that education is something being done to them, often by adults who are not enjoying themselves. For students to be engaged, they need to feel known by the adults around them and that they have advocates working to help them succeed."

—Arthur Baraf, Principal, The Met High School (2019, p. 362)

Ideally, engagement should not be a contested space where one party wins at the expense of the other, nor should it be a situation where both parties lose at the expense of both engagement and learning. The evidence is clear on the effectiveness of trying to force students to engage. When we try to control students and their engagement in learning activities, we might be successful in getting some students to a level of compliance, but this is a far cry from being highly invested and motivated to learn. Controlling approaches are often experienced as demotivating rather than motivating—not what we want if we are aiming for students to get to the *driving* level of engagement.

There is an alternative, of course. If the goal is to see all students make progress and to support them to become highly motivated learners who have the skills and the will to drive their learning, then we need to remove the battle lines and join forces.

partnership (n)

A relationship between individuals or groups that is characterized by mutual cooperation and responsibility, as for the achievement of a specified goal.

A misconception that I have come up against in my work with teachers is that the more active and engaged students become, the less active and engaged teachers become. If you've ever had the pleasure of observing a classroom where the students are highly engaged in what they are doing, you might be familiar with the real "buzz" of energy and the productive hum as students share their ideas, celebrate sudden insights, and put their heads together to decide what to do next. In this situation, we teach less, and they learn more. You may also be familiar with the expert teacher who is equally engaged in the class-room discussions, called in by students to witness the latest achievement, and sought out to offer suggestions or feedback on where to go next. These teachers and their students are active partners in the learning process, and both are highly engaged in what they are doing.

In a partnership, teachers and students come together to work toward a common goal, with both parties sharing the responsibility for engagement (and success). This is in contrast to more commonly held ideas that have the teacher pushing or pulling students in the direction the teacher wants them to go, and the students either agreeing to go along with it or resisting these attempts. As partners in engagement, both teacher and student have important roles to play and bring valuable resources and skills to maximize engagement in learning.

As we create our foundation for engagement, one of the first things we can do is to identify whether we are on the path of battling over student engagement or on the path of partnering for engagement. Quite possibly, there are elements of both in your classroom. Sometimes we praise and welcome those who are engaged and come up with explanations for why others are not. Sometimes we fall into a pattern with some students that feels like a constant battle, but with others, it feels like we are more in sync. It can also depend on the day and the activity. For example, some students might willingly participate in one subject but actively resist getting involved in another. This variability is one of the challenges of student engagement, as one teacher described it:

"I have some students who are consistently there—present, engaged, ready to go all the time. Then there are those who fluctuate. They can have great weeks, they can have great hours, and they can have a great fifteen minutes. I'm always navigating that."

Importantly, just because students are *participating* in the activity you have planned does not mean that they are motivated to learn. They may be passively complying to avoid conflict or simply because it is the easiest path for getting through the lesson. If we are aiming for higher levels of engagement—*investing* and *driving*—then students will need to be motivated enough to want to put in the effort needed to learn and skilled enough to take actions that will see them make progress in learning. It's at these higher levels that a partnership model will provide a more productive pathway for engagement.

Where there are signs of a partnership in place, then we can focus on building on those foundations. If, however, you find yourself in a situation where you are either facing a battle of wills over engagement or coming up against a ceiling of passive compliance, then it may be time to reimagine engagement and start to plot a different path forward.

TIME TO REFLECT

Thinking about your experiences—both as a teacher and as a student—can you identify examples of the "battle" over engagement?

Have you had experiences—both as a teacher and as a student—of willing compliance that might be categorized as *participating*? As a learner, have you ever been in a situation where you felt like you were working with someone in a way that inspired you to become highly *invested* in what you were learning or to want to *drive* your learning even further?

Have you had any experiences as a teacher where you felt like you were in a collaborative partnership with students as they became highly *invested* in learning and actively engaged in *driving* their learning even further?

WHAT CAN TEACHERS BRING TO THE ENGAGEMENT PARTNERSHIP?

In a partnership model, teachers play an integral role in supporting students to reach the level of engagement described in *driving*. This includes designing learning experiences that aim to optimize engagement, energizing students' inner motivational resources, supporting student autonomy and agency, collaborating with all students to optimize engagement, and cultivating a culture of engagement.

Let's look at these different aspects of supporting student engagement. We will continue to explore them in the chapters that follow.

DESIGNING LEARNING EXPERIENCES THAT OPTIMIZE ENGAGEMENT

It may seem obvious, but if we are aiming for students to move along the continuum from *participating* to *driving*, then we need to design learning experiences that require the level of effort described in *driving*. For example, the task needs to be sufficiently challenging and open enough to justify conversations about improving or making progress toward a goal—not just getting the answers correct or finishing on time. In other words, the focus for *driving* is on learning rather than doing (*participating*). This does not mean that there isn't a place for activities that develop important foundational knowledge and skills, but it does mean that we do this with the intent of taking the learning and engagement deeper and increasing the challenge over time—and we share this intent with the students.

A killer of enhanced engagement is asking students to do more of the same when they have completed an activity. In his book *The Joy of Not Knowing*, Marcello Staricoff (2021) discusses the motivational value of turning up the challenge once students have mastered a skill or concept, rather than assigning "more of the same" type of tasks. He recounted an example of a Grade 5 class spending a week mastering the grid method for multiplication, then applying that method to tackle a HOTS (higher-order thinking skills) challenge where they had to estimate how much revenue a local bridge made in a year from people paying to cross. In this example, the students were able to participate in activities that asked them to practice the grid method, but then move beyond that to take on a challenge that had them collaborating with their peers toward a shared goal that required them to use the grid method over and over again as they tried to find an answer to a real-world problem.

When we are designing learning experiences, we do so with both engagement and learning in mind. This means we are considering the level of challenge, connecting learning experiences with the aim of moving from surface to deep, and building in opportunities for collaboration and social interaction within the learning experience as a key feature of *investing* and *driving*. We will look at this in more detail in Chapters 3 and 4 when we explore the differences in expectations for engagement as students take on increasing levels of challenge, and in Chapter 6 when we talk about engaging with peers to learn.

ENERGIZING STUDENTS' INNER MOTIVATIONAL RESOURCES

Motivation researchers describe three basic psychological needs that provide the fundamental foundation and fuel for active engagement in learning and well-being in general. These are the need for *autonomy*, *competence*, and *relatedness* (Deci & Ryan, 2000). Each of these needs can be supported or thwarted at school, leading to feelings of either satisfaction or frustration. When our need for *autonomy* is met, we feel like we are able and willing to make meaningful choices and decisions, and are free to think, act, and feel without being pressured or controlled by someone else. If this need is frustrated, we can feel in conflict, like we are being pushed or pulled in a direction we might not want to go—as we have seen in the battle for engagement. Rather than trying to control student engagement, we aim to take an autonomy-supportive approach that enlists students as engagement partners and empowers them to make decisions and have a say about their engagement in learning. We will explore this in more detail shortly, but first, let's look at the need for *competence* and *relatedness*.

The need for *competence* is satisfied when we can effectively engage in opportunities that allow us to extend ourselves, experience success, and feel like we've mastered something. If this need is frustrated, we can feel like we are a failure or incapable of success. It is not hard to see why students who experience little or no success while at school might choose to disengage from activities and classroom learning experiences. After all, who wants to put their hand up for yet another opportunity to fail publicly while others around them are succeeding? Better to opt out altogether. Importantly, it is not about only ever doing things we know we can do well—this can get boring and doesn't provide us with the opportunity to develop resilience and strategies for dealing with setbacks and failures. Challenge can provide the fuel and motivation that we need to become actively engaged and driven to succeed. As teachers, it is important to identify the right amount of challenge—too little and it could be boring with limited chance to learn; too much and the students are unlikely to succeed or progress in their learning.

Finally, the need for *relatedness* is satisfied when we feel connected to and valued by others. When our need for related-ness is not met, we can experience feelings of being alienated, excluded, and lonely. Learning, particularly in the context of school, is a social activity, and relationships are at the core of student engagement. There is a large body of evidence showing that the teacher–student relationship, no matter the age of the students, is associated with both engagement and achievement, and these relationships may be especially important for students who are academically at risk due to learning difficulties or socioeconomic disadvantage (Roorda et al., 2011).

Building positive relationships with our students may begin with showing that we care for them, that we are interested in them, that we listen and show we understand what we are hearing from them, and that we respect them, but being likable is not enough to improve student learning. There are other aspects to the relationship that we need to attend to as well, including the quality of our instruction and the structure and support that we provide to students as they learn. Our role is to demonstrate that we not only care about each student but we also believe in their potential to learn, have high expectations for them, and are there to provide the support and structure that will enable them to achieve success and make progress in their learning. In short, we need to become as engaged in the engagement partnership as the student is.

"Students who perceive teachers as creating a caring, well-structured learning environment in which expectations are high, clear, and fair are more likely to report engagement in school."

—Adena Klem and James Connell (2004, p. 270)

In addition to these basic psychological needs, students come equipped with other motivational resources that can fuel engagement. These include their interests, curiosity, and goals they have for themselves. These interests, goals, and capacity to be curious often need to be stretched by the teacher, communicating the message that we see excitement, curiosity, opportunities, and expectations in them above their own beliefs about themselves. So, our role is to build on existing interests *and* develop new interests in things they may not have experienced or liked before, develop a culture of asking "why" questions as these are the essence of curiosity, and show them that we have high expectations for their learning and believe in their ability to realize higher expectations of their learning than they previously thought possible. Our role is not to help them realize what they *think* is their potential but to offer them greater potential and show we can help them to realize that potential.

The interactions that we have with students and the learning activities that we design can either involve and energize students' inner motivational resources or frustrate and demotivate them.

SUPPORTING STUDENT AUTONOMY AND AGENCY

When students are operating at the *driving* level of engagement, they are infused with a sense of autonomy and acting with agency. That is, they are feeling in control of their learning, know what to do when they do not know what to do, and are confident to take action in pursuit of the goals they have set for themselves. As teachers, we can support student autonomy and agency or act in ways that frustrate autonomy and inhibit agency.

WHAT DOES THE RESEARCH SAY?

Johnmarshall Reeve has been studying student engagement and motivation for over two decades. He describes two approaches teachers take to motivating and engaging students. At one end of the continuum is a highly autonomy-supportive style, and at the other end is a highly controlling style, with a range of different combinations in between. Essentially, highly controlling teachers operate in a way that says, "I am the boss. I will tell you what to do, what to think, and how to feel." In contrast, the way that highly autonomy-supportive teachers interact with students says, "I am your ally. I am here to support you and help you reach your goals."

The evidence on the impact of these two approaches is clear: Students benefit from autonomy support and suffer from being controlled. The benefits of an autonomy-supportive approach include improvements in motivation, engagement, learning, achievement, and well-being. In contrast, a controlling approach undermines student motivation, focuses on compliance rather than deeper engagement, and prevents students from realizing the benefits to learning and well-being that come from being highly motivated, acting with agency, and engaging deeply in classroom learning experiences (Reeve, 2009).

While we may not set out to be controlling, it remains that this type of motivating style is alive and well in K–12 classrooms. There are many reasons why a teacher might adopt this type of approach—for example, equating controlling strategies with being a competent teacher who is responsible for managing classroom activities and student behavior, and a misconception that autonomy-supportive strategies equate to "letting them do whatever they want." Sometimes teachers are pulled into a controlling style when faced with students who appear unmotivated, passive, or disengaged. Teachers' beliefs about student motivation can also position them toward a more controlling style—for example, believing that offering rewards is a more effective strategy for getting students to engage than explaining the rationale behind the planned activity (Reeve, 2009, 2016).

It is powerful and easier to be controlling if the goal is passive *participating*. This entails surveillance, discipline, and making the work readily attainable (not stretching or challenging the students). What is fascinating is that some high-achieving students find much comfort in teachers controlling the learning for them. This is the game they are good at, get praise for, and like as the focus is simply on "doing" what the teacher asks for. Some students dislike unstructured problems, wading into the learning pit of the unknown, and the uneasiness of the chaos of learning. They are compliance junkies, and while this may serve them well for some years, when they confront new domains, face new challenges, and are asked to reach new heights, they can falter. No wonder most gifted students do not become gifted adults. They are still at the "doing" stage and have not learned to move to the *investing* and *driving* stages of learning other than in their areas of expertise.

The autonomy-supportive approach sits at the heart of our engagement partnership, enabling students to move from *participating* to *driving*. While a controlling approach may pressure students into a level of compliance, this passive form of engagement lacks the inner motivational fuel that is needed to reach the *investing* and *driving* levels of engagement.

So how do we know if we are being autonomy-supportive or controlling? Reeve (2016) describes six different instructional behaviors that are associated with the autonomy-supportive approach and the opposing behavior that represents a controlling approach:

Autonomy-Supportive	Controlling
Taking the students' perspective	Taking only the teacher's perspective
Energizing students' inner motivational resources (e.g., curiosity, interest, autonomy)	Introducing extrinsic motivators (e.g., incentives, consequences)
Explaining the value, benefit, or reason for requests, rules, procedures, and uninteresting activities	Neglecting to provide an explanation or reason
Using nonpressuring language (e.g., offering choices)	Using controlling, pressuring language
Acknowledging and accepting negative responses or emotions	Arguing with or trying to change negative reactions or emotions
Displaying patience— allowing students to work at their own pace and in their own way	Displaying impatience— rushing students to get it right, get it done quickly, taking over

In the following chapters, we will continue to revisit the concept of supporting student autonomy and agency as an important part of the role of the teacher.

TIME TO REFLECT

While we may not set out to be intentionally controlling, chances are we've all acted in a controlling way at some time in the classroom. The first step to becoming more autonomy-supportive is to become aware of the ways that we are being controlling and try to reduce that. Then we can try to increase our autonomy-supportive behaviors. If we accept that we all might fall into controlling behavior from time to time, then one thing we can do is to identify the things that push or pull us toward this kind of approach. Perhaps it is certain student behaviors that trigger us—for example, students who are demonstrating *avoiding*-type behaviors rather than engaging in a planned learning activity. For others, it might be the sense of pressure to get through the prescribed content or achieve certain outputs in the lesson. Or, it might be our own beliefs about the best way to motivate or engage students that sends us down the path of controlling rather than autonomy support.

CULTIVATING A CULTURE OF ENGAGEMENT

Operating at the *driving* level is all about seeking out challenges, setting goals for improvement, and striving toward something. Unfortunately, this often runs counter to the existing norms and "rules of the game" at school. Many students have learned that being successful at school means getting the correct answer (and quickly!), getting things done, and getting things in on time. This type of culture rewards compliance and does not invite risk-taking, mistake-making, or challenge-seeking. Assuming students have the necessary ability and care enough about the game of school, success is achievable if they just do what the teacher asks of them. If this is the culture of the school that students are used to, then we may need to begin our engagement partnership by cultivating a new culture—one of engagement, embracing challenges, and striving to improve. Not all students will willingly embrace challenge or come equipped with the skills and motivation needed to successfully drive their own learning. Some children have had so few experiences of success in the classroom that they will want to actively avoid any challenge as yet another experience of not knowing or not being able to. Others might be used to winning at the game of school by getting things done quickly and getting things right with limited effort. These students may resist our attempts to change the rules of the game on them as it means more effort for them and brings the possibility of mistakes and failure. In Chapter 7, we will look at building a culture of engagement where we celebrate mistakes and embrace challenge as we chase the thrill of success and progress after a period of struggle.

TAKING IT INTO THE CLASSROOM

Wondering what your students think the culture of the school is? Why not ask them and find out? This can be a first step in inviting them to become partners in learning and engagement as you look at learning from their perspective. You might ask these questions:

- What do good learners do?
- What does it mean to be a successful learner at school?
- What does it mean when you make a mistake or get things wrong? How does it make you feel?
- What helps you to learn at school?
- What makes it hard for you to learn?

You can do this as a class discussion or seek student input in more anonymous ways such as sticky notes.

You could also use an online tool such as Google Jamboard or Padlet to invite students to share their thoughts and feelings.

The responses you receive can give you great insight into the existing culture in your classroom and help you to identify elements you can build on and grow, as well as things that might require a shift in thinking as we cultivate a culture that optimizes engagement.

Part of our culture means having a shared language for engagement and a process for thinking about and talking about engagement in learning, providing the necessary structure and support students need to act with agency and a sense of autonomy, competence, and relatedness. The continuum of engagement presented in Chapter 1 provides teachers and students with a common language for discussing engagement, one that goes beyond simply *engaged* or *disengaged*. It gives us easily observed behaviors that are characteristic of the different forms of engagement, helping us to create intentions for engagement and criteria for monitoring engagement and describing different engagement pathways for learning. While some may believe that providing this kind of structure is at odds with supporting student autonomy, this is a misconception. The evidence suggests that providing both structure and autonomy support is the most effective pathway to the kind of active, self-regulated engagement described in *driving* (Cheon et al., 2020; Sierens et al., 2009). Teachers can provide structure in an autonomy-supportive way by communicating clear expectations for engagement and learning, setting transparent criteria for success, and introducing clearly defined processes and procedures for engaging in learning. In the next chapter, we will look at a process for embedding engagement within the learning experience so that it becomes a part of our classroom learning culture—or "how we do things around here." This process is a collaborative one, in the spirit of our engagement partnership, rather than something we do to students.

COLLABORATING WITH ALL STUDENTS TO OPTIMIZE ENGAGEMENT

Another misconception about engagement is that teachers only have to support certain students to engage—or, more accurately, help them to "do" the activity and, in particular, to support those identified as "unmotivated" or at lower ability levels. By this deficit view, only some students need the help of the teacher, and the rest can manage to get engaged and stay engaged without the help of the teacher. The problem with this type of thinking is it can go hand in hand with a view of engagement that sits at the *participating* level and a controlling rather than autonomy-supportive approach. In other words, it takes us back to the battle for compliance rather than a partnership for engagement. In contrast, we are actively collaborating with *all* students to maximize their engagement and learning. That means we seek their input and think about things from their perspective during planning, and during learning we seek feedback from them about their engagement and learning; we develop a shared understanding of what engagement looks like and the different engagement pathways that lead to learning. Getting to know each of our students will help us to better understand their individual engagement patterns, the things that help them to engage, and the things that lead them to disengage.

This partnership for engagement extends beyond the teacher and student, allowing students to become engagement partners for each other as well. When we look at what students bring to the engagement partnership, we will see that they are active collaborators in this process, providing valuable inputs into their engagement and the engagement of others.

WHAT CAN STUDENTS BRING TO THE ENGAGEMENT PARTNERSHIP?

With all the talk of "hooking students in," "getting students engaged," and "keeping students engaged," we might be forgiven for thinking that a student's only role in engagement is to be pushed or pulled by the teacher in the direction the teacher wants them to go, like a pawn in a game rather than a valued teammate. Thinking about student engagement in this way, it is the teacher who is responsible for thinking about engagement, deciding what constitutes "being engaged," monitoring engagement, and stepping in to take control when students aren't meeting the expectations for engagement—not much of a partnership.

Reimagining the teacher's role in student engagement is one piece of the puzzle, but we also need to consider the implications for students and what can be expected of them in this new approach. After all, if we are going to share the responsibility for engagement, then everyone needs to know what that involves. So, what can students bring to the engagement partnership?

INVESTING MOTIVATION AND EFFORT

We've already discussed the rich inner motivational resources that students bring into the classroom; these are the fuel for engagement in learning should the student decide to invest them. They include feelings of having autonomy over their learning, feeling competent and able to achieve success, feeling connected and valued by those within the learning environment, feeling interested or curious about what is being learned, and having a sense that the learning is personally meaningful or valuable. Along with motivation to learn, students also bring the effort that is needed to make progress and improve. How much effort they invest will depend on their motivation and the task itself. When the inner motivation is not sufficiently energized, it will be hard to move beyond a state of passive, compliant *participation*. If the challenge level of the task is too low, it will be easy for students to take the strategic path and "coast" with limited effort or choose to disengage because it is too boring. If the challenge is too great, students may opt out rather than risking embarrassment and frustration and wasting effort on something unlikely to lead to success.

In short, students contribute to the engagement partnership by choosing to invest their motivational resources and effort as they strive to make progress in their learning.

TAKING AGENCY OVER
ENGAGEMENT AND LEARNING

Students' input into the engagement partnership goes beyond deciding if they will engage and to what extent. Students are also capable of actively influencing the learning environment to benefit both their motivation and learning. They do this by proactively communicating their interests, needs, and preferences for learning; taking steps to seek support and make progress in their learning; and working in collaboration with others in ways that benefit their motivation and learning (Reeve et al., 2020). If you think this sounds a lot like the *driving* form of engagement, you're right!

Communicating

When students take agency by communicating their needs, interests, and preferences, teachers tend to respond in increasingly autonomy-supportive ways (Matos et al., 2018). That is, when students proactively share what they are interested in learning, how they prefer to learn, and the things that they need to progress in their learning, teachers are more inclined to listen to their ideas, provide choices and options for students, encourage them to ask questions and communicate about their learning, and show confidence in their ability to succeed. We have already seen that an autonomy-supportive approach is beneficial to student engagement, but this is not a one-way street from teacher to student. It seems that students who demonstrate and communicate active engagement in what they are learning can influence the teacher to be increasingly supportive of their autonomy—which in turn will continue to energize student motivation and engagement.

SNAPSHOT OF PRACTICE

One of the teachers I interviewed, Nicole, explained this beautifully. The teaching team had planned an inquiry unit focusing on social justice that was meant to go for one term but ended up being extended based on the engagement of the students:

"We only planned the inquiry to go for a term, but we ended up taking it over two terms because it just took on a life of its own. The kids were asking questions and wanting to research different community organizations. They wanted to take it further. They said, 'We can actually do something to make a difference and get out there.' So, we decided to carry it over and took it into Term 3. They

(Continued)

(Continued)

chose the organization they wanted to research, figured out how they could help, and worked together as teams to pull it off. They'd come in first thing in the morning talking about it, asking when they were going to get time to plan. I got really excited about it too, and invested in what they were doing."

By communicating their interest in taking the planned inquiry unit further, and asking for things they needed to progress—like time to plan and space to meet with their groups—these students were able to influence the teacher's plans and create a learning experience that was highly motivating and extended their understanding of the concept of social justice and their place in the community.

Taking Action to Learn

The students in Nicole's class did more than just communicate their needs, ideas, and interests to her; they were also taking action and steps to help them move forward. They identified meaningful goals for extending their learning, made plans for reaching those goals, asked questions and looked for the answers using the research skills they had been taught, and reflected on their discoveries and plans along the way. Far from just waiting to be told what to do, these students were taking their learning into their own hands. When students are taking action to learn, they understand what they are trying to achieve, have a path in mind to get them to that goal, and seek support along the way when needed. These behaviors are indicative of students being in *driving* mode and include several strategies that have the potential to considerably accelerate student achievement according to Visible Learning Meta[x] (www.visiblelearningmetax.com)— for example, help-seeking, self-judgment and reflection, self-directed learning, and effort management. A key to taking action is having the right strategies and being able to use them effectively to make progress. To keep the internal flames of motivation going, students need to feel like they are entrusted to make decisions about their learning (including the decision to seek help from others when needed), but also confident that they are capable of achieving success and making progress when doing so.

Collaborating With Others

One action students can take to benefit both their engagement and learning is to collaborate with others. When students choose to collaborate with the teacher or with their peers, they are actively seeking a partner who will help them manage their motivation, engagement, and learning. This might include seeking feedback on their ideas or input on where to go next:

> *"They were seeking extension for themselves, seeking challenges—you know, coming up to me asking, 'What can I do next?' or 'Would this be a good route to take?' and 'What do you think about this question? Do you think this would be a good idea?'"*

The collaboration extends beyond help-seeking, though. At times, students share their discoveries, expertise, and insights—often to the benefit of the teacher's own engagement:

> *"I really enjoy having the kids come up to me so excited to explain what they've done or something they've just discovered—it's often so much better than I expected. I love learning new things from them. It's like we're switching roles and they are the experts. Especially with some of my kids who really struggle and then they're able to be an expert on something and they're teaching someone something new. It's fantastic!"*

Of course, students also have peers they can collaborate with. At the *investing* level, students are eager to share their ideas and thinking with peers. They might also decide to pair up with others who have similar interests during an activity. At the *driving* level, students are actively collaborating with others toward a shared goal and challenging each other to drive improvement and progress.

> *"I think the questioning is a big thing. If I hear kids questioning each other and, you know, debating issues and sharing opinions and that sort of thing, that's a higher level of engagement. It's not just a passive listening to somebody and then taking my turn to say what I think. It's actually adding to what they've said, and challenging what's been said. 'Yes, and what about this?' or 'Have you considered this?'"*

LET'S GET THIS PARTNERSHIP STARTED!

As we enter into the engagement partnership, each party must understand what is expected of them. To briefly summarize what each can contribute to student engagement:

Teachers can:

- Design learning experiences that optimize engagement

- Energize students' inner motivational resources

Students can:

- Invest their motivation and effort into learning

- Communicate their interests, ideas, preferences, and needs

- Support student autonomy and agency

- Cultivate a culture of engagement

- Collaborate with all students to optimize engagement

- Take action to engage in learning and make progress

- **Collaborate to benefit engagement and learning**

We could just put this up on the board and tell students, "This is what you have to do," but that would be at odds with all that we've learned in this chapter. In the spirit of autonomy support and seeking the active input of our partners, you might like to do as Nicole did with her Grade 5 and 6 students. Before our interview, she was reflecting on her thinking about student engagement and found she was interested in hearing what the students had to say about it. She wanted to find out how their perspective compared to her own, but also as a way of getting feedback on their engagement and her teaching. The students ran the discussion themselves, recording the responses on a T-chart with "What engages us" on one side and "What disengages us" on the other. Nicole found the responses to be very insightful and helped her to understand her students' perspectives on their engagement. Some of the comments that came out of the discussion include the following:

"Working with people you wouldn't normally work with because when I work with my friends it's a lot easier to be distracted, so I'm not as engaged. When I have to work with someone else, I'm really listening to what they're saying because I'm not used to who they are and how they work."

"How you introduce the lesson. I'll be either engaged from the beginning or I'll have to work to stay engaged."

"Let me try it first before you come and help. I become disengaged if I find out the answer too quickly."

Try it with your students. It can give you an insight into their perspective, and they might surprise you with what they have to say!

CHAPTER 3

Developing a Process for Engagement

"Why don't we have students set their intention today [for engagement], instead of getting angry or frustrated when learners don't engage? Rather than trying to bribe them with points and things, what if we actually taught learners, 'This is what engagement looks like,' and then invited them to set their intention for the day—'What is going to be your level of engagement?'—and then encouraged them to reflect, 'What was your level of engagement, and how do you know? Do you have any evidence?'"

—Doug Fisher on using the engagement continuum (Corwin, 2021)

Now that we understand how teachers and students actively contribute to the engagement partnership, we turn our attention to embedding engagement within the teaching and learning process. As you will recall from Chapter 1, our focus in this book is optimizing student engagement in classroom learning activities (rather than engagement in school more broadly). It makes sense then that we would look for ways to explicitly connect our thinking and discussions around engagement with our thinking and discussions around learning. After all, when students are engaged in the planned learning experience, we hope that means they are on the pathway to progress and learning.

Previous research tells us teachers are pretty good at determining if students are engaged or disengaged during learning, but less effective at deciding what to do about it (Skinner & Pitzer, 2012). Unsurprisingly, teachers are better at judging the observable aspects of engagement, like being on task, but not as accurate in their judgments of the more hidden aspects such as inner motivations (e.g., seeing the value in a learning activity; Lee & Reeve, 2012). As teachers, we may believe that it is our responsibility to make sure our students are engaged, but trying to take it all on ourselves might not be the best path. This type of thinking brings us back to the old model where the teacher is expected to decide how the students will engage, figure out if students are engaged, and try to engage or reengage them during a lesson. Several teachers I talked to expressed a lack of confidence in their ability to successfully take this on:

> *"Engagement can be really hard to figure out, because are they engaged, or are they just there? Sometimes you don't know. They might look like they're engaged, they might look like they're looking at you, and they might have good body language, but are they actually interested in what you're talking about, interested in learning? That's the thing— to try to figure out how can I make them care and make them want to learn? But I don't know that I have the capacity to make them. Do I have the ability to make someone care about learning? Probably not."*

SHARING RESPONSIBILITY FOR ENGAGEMENT AND LEARNING

In our partnership model, we don't rely only on our interpretations and guesswork to understand what is going on or how to improve the engagement of our students. Instead, we share the responsibility with students and invite them to collaborate with us as active partners in engagement. As a start, this involves establishing a shared language for discussing and thinking about engagement, using the engagement continuum as our foundation.

SNAPSHOT OF PRACTICE

I was recently watching a presentation given by Doug Fisher and John Hattie (Corwin, 2021). Doug started the presentation by talking about engagement and the importance of working with students on engagement: having conversations about engagement, setting intentions for engagement, and reflecting on engagement—all using the continuum of engagement. Doug showed a video of Thomas's classroom where the students were engaged in a jigsaw activity focused on the six forms of engagement from the continuum. The aim of the activity, as Thomas explained to the students, was to get to a place where they could self-assess their level of engagement using the language from the continuum. The students were actively engaged in the discussions, explaining what each form of engagement meant to them and using examples from the classroom and their own experiences to illustrate what they meant. They were even able to explain the differences between different forms, noting that *avoiding* involved an active, purposeful decision to not do the work while *withdrawing* was a more passive loss of interest in the activity. Through this activity, the students in Thomas's class were able to situate the continuum, and the different forms of engagement, within the real-world context of their classroom using examples and descriptions that were both relevant and meaningful to them. Even more, they were able to reflect on and describe the things that helped them to operate at the *driving* level, such as having success criteria and good time management skills. Now that Thomas's students understand the language of engagement, each day they are asked to set their intentions for engagement at the beginning of the lesson and then reflect on their level of engagement in an exit slip at the end of the lesson.

In addition to a shared language for engagement, we need a process for setting intentions for engagement, monitoring and reflecting on engagement, making adjustments to improve engagement, and deciding on the next steps for engaging in learning. This process is designed to support student autonomy and agency, communicate to students that we value their input and believe in their ability to make progress, show them they need to also be responsible for investing in the learning, and provide the necessary structure for students to become masters of their engagement and learning. As we learned in Chapter 2, these are all linked to students' inner motivational resources—making the process part of energizing motivation and fueling engagement.

If you are familiar with common models for formative assessment or formative evaluation, you may see a similarity with the process outlined in this chapter. Both are focused on improvement, are embedded in everyday teaching and learning, and position teachers and students as co-collaborators who share the responsibility for learning. Paul Black and Dylan Wiliam (2009), well known for their work on formative assessment, described the three key components that make up the formative assessment cycle:

Process	Strategies
Establishing where the learner is going	Learning intentions and success criteria
Finding out where the learner is right now	Questioning, classroom discussion, learning tasks
Identifying a path for moving forward	Feedback, self-assessment, peer assessment

Formative assessment (or formative evaluation as some prefer) has been identified as "one of the most powerful ways to enhance student motivation and achievement" (Cauley & McMillan, 2010). Using strategies such as clear learning intentions and success criteria, and providing feedback that helps students move forward, means there is less confusion about what they are learning and what the pathway to learning looks like. This supports students to act with agency and proceed with confidence that they are capable of success. To maximize the benefit to student motivation and engagement, teachers should support students to become actively involved in the process, setting their own goals for improvement and monitoring their progress.

The benefits of formative assessment strategies for student engagement have been widely discussed, but what about introducing an explicit focus on engagement into the process? That is, what if we had a dual focus on both learning and engagement when planning, monitoring, and evaluating student progress? As we have already looked into the different ways that teachers and students contribute to the engagement partnership, now we will situate that within the context of the teaching and learning process.

DESIGNING FOR OPTIMUM ENGAGEMENT

When we design a learning experience that supports optimum engagement, there are several things we need to consider, including how the experience will energize the students' inner motivational resources, how the experience will provide the right level of challenge, and what barriers might put students on a path to disengagement. Of course, we want all of our lessons to be optimally engaging, but it can help to think beyond an individual lesson and consider how students might be supported to move from *participating* to *driving* over a series of lessons. When we focus only on the level of one lesson, it is easy to remain fixated on what we need to "get through," and what the students need to "get done." Instead, we want to elevate our expectations and look ahead to where we want students to "get to" in their engagement and learning.

SNAPSHOT OF PRACTICE

In my interviews, I asked teachers how they planned for engagement and what kind of things they thought about when planning for engagement. Many teachers talked about ways to "hook" students in or make learning more interesting for students. There were some, though, who bravely admitted that engagement wasn't something that was front of mind when they sat down to plan:

"If I'm being totally honest, I probably just look at the topic, think about what I need to get through, and say quickly, 'I'm going to just do it like I usually do it.' When it actually comes to me in front of the class, though, then I gauge their interest level, and if I see that some of them are starting to get restless or not interested, then I look for ways to mix it up and change it. But in the actual planning . . . my forward thinking is not really about how I'm going to engage them; it's what I'm going to teach and what's the outcome. So, that's when I start changing things around a little bit when I'm actually working with them."

It is easy to understand how teachers can get stuck in this mode. Teaching is busy, and the pressure to plan lessons, get through content from the curriculum, get the learners to a certain standard, and achieve a certain level of output is often high. However, it is this kind of thinking that can put us on a dangerous path for battle as it does little to energize student motivation to learn.

WHAT CAN TEACHERS DO?

Take a backward design approach when planning for engagement. When planning for engagement, begin by thinking about the goal of students *driving* their learning. At the *driving* level, students are striving to improve and make progress in their understanding or skills, and driven to achieve a personally meaningful goal. They are taking action, acting with agency, and interacting with others to support this progress. With that in mind, what would it look like with the intended focus for learning? For example, if students are learning to write a narrative that other people will enjoy reading, what would they be doing at the *driving* level? They might be asking a friend for suggestions on one of their characters, agreeing to swap stories with a peer and give each other feedback, or collaborating with someone to coauthor a story. Or, they might be reading through their work and identifying things that don't make sense, and asking you for feedback on an idea they have for making the story more interesting. When we start to consider the end goal in terms of engagement, then we can start to think of ways to activate and energize this type of engagement. We can also think about the series of lessons and activities that might connect and support students to act with increasing agency, collaborate more effectively, and take on increasing challenges as they move from *participating* to *driving*.

Seek input from students during planning. This could include getting information about their interests, things they are curious about, what they already know and can do, and potential roadblocks to engagement that might stem from their previous experiences with the subject, concepts, or skills—for example, students' feelings about writing, their understanding of a concept, or their interest in a current issue in the news. As autonomy-supportive teachers, we accept and acknowledge negative responses, we listen to students' ideas and suggestions, and we remain flexible and ready to adapt or adjust our plans based on the input from students to benefit motivation, engagement, and learning. Importantly, it does no good to gather information from students if we don't do something with that information. In the case of engagement, the aim of seeking student input is to use that information to inform our decision making about the next steps for teaching, learning, and engagement.

WHAT CAN STUDENTS DO?

While it is true that teachers are ultimately responsible for connecting students with the content of the curriculum and taking on the heavy lifting of planning for this, students have important contributions to make to this process—if we are prepared to listen.

Share their interests, questions, and ideas. One thing that students can do is to communicate with the teacher about the planned learning experience and pathway for learning. This includes sharing the things they are interested in learning more about or want to do better, sharing the questions they have or the things they are curious about, and suggesting ideas for improving the planned learning experience to make it more engaging. Making this a regular part of the process, providing students with strategies for sharing, and providing regular opportunities to share (not just during planning) can help them to become more confident in taking on this role, and more able to identify areas of personal interest, ask good questions, and come up with different ideas for making the learning more engaging. Showing students we are genuinely interested in their input, and willing to act on their ideas and suggestions, will help demonstrate our commitment to the partnership.

Identify things that help them engage and things that might cause them to disengage. Rather than relying on the teacher to come up with ways to engage them, students can contribute by providing their ideas and insights. For example, some students might prefer to have more scaffolding to start with as they work up the confidence to take on a challenge, while others might prefer to jump straight in and try as a way of figuring out what they can do and what they might need help with. Getting in touch with their inner motivational resources, and understanding their patterns of engaging and disengaging, may take time and practice, but with your support and scaffolding, they can become experts on their engagement. We will look at this in more detail in Chapters 4 and 5.

TIME TO REFLECT

When it comes to engagement, what do you think about when you are planning? Do you plan with engagement in mind?

Looking at the ideas for teachers and students, what are you already doing? What other ideas could you try with your students?

THE PROCESS—ESTABLISHING THE RULES OF ENGAGEMENT

In a talk hosted by the National Research Council's Center for Education, Lee Shulman (2005) described *signature pedagogies* of different professions like law and medicine, where the way of teaching is explicitly focused on preparing students for that profession—that is, teaching them not only to "do" what doctors or lawyers do, but also to "think like a lawyer" or "think like a doctor." A characteristic of these highly engaging signature pedagogies is that the rules of engagement are clear and everyone knows them because they are habitual and routine. Everyone is kept on their toes, with all students visible (no flying under the radar!), and the processes of questioning, thinking, and responding are visible, too, as medical students go on hospital rounds and law students go through the cases of the day. Students are accountable not only to the teacher but to each other as well, and a necessary degree of engagement is built in with an emphasis on taking action, not just taking in information. As Shulman noted, these routine processes and protocols for engaging build "habits of mind" and "habits of the heart," because they bring together ways of thinking and reasoning with the development of identity, values, and being connected with others in learning.

If we were to apply the idea of a signature pedagogy to our work in the classroom, what might it look like? How might we teach students to "think like a learner" rather than emphasizing the "doing" aspects of being a student—doing the work, following instructions, and being compliant? One way to do this is to make the process of thinking and talking about engagement both visible and habitual so that everyone knows the rules of engagement and everyone is accountable for their engagement and the engagement of the group. The process described in the following section has three components: *setting intentions for engagement*, *checking in on engagement*, and *planning the next steps for engagement*. The process is designed to sit alongside a practice of setting intentions and success criteria for learning, establishing where students are in their learning, and deciding on the next steps for learning.

HOW WILL I ENGAGE IN LEARNING? SETTING INTENTIONS FOR ENGAGEMENT

You may be familiar with the use of learning intentions and success criteria, and may already use them in your classroom. When we set intentions for learning, we are describing what we want students to know and be able to do as a result of the learning experience. For example:

In this chapter, we are learning about how to embed engagement within the teaching and learning process.

Sometimes people mistakenly confuse the teacher's intentions for what the students will be *doing* (e.g., We are using pictures to retell the story of *Elmer the Elephant*) with the intentions for *learning* (e.g., We are learning about the different parts of a story). Intentions for *doing* are generally tied to one activity or one lesson, whereas intentions for *learning* can spread across multiple lessons and involve many different activities.

Setting clear intentions for learning gives students valuable information about where they are going and what they are working toward; describing what success will look like (in the form of success criteria) allows them to know when they get there.

This practice can contribute to students' inner motivational resources by providing the tools they need to manage their progress (supporting autonomy) and a clear pathway for learning that helps them to feel that success is within their control (supporting competence). We can extend this practice to include intentions for engagement and criteria to describe different engagement pathways.

INTENTIONS FOR ENGAGEMENT

When we talk about intentions for engagement, we are looking to identify the level of engagement that will be invested toward the learning intention. The continuum provides us with a useful reference point in the form of the three levels of engaging: *participating*, *investing*, and *driving*. As we want our students to take ownership over their engagement, they will be actively involved in setting their intentions for engaging in learning and evaluating their engagement during learning. To support them in this, we can describe the different engagement pathways that relate to the three levels of engagement. What will it look like when students are on the *participating pathway*? What do they need to be doing to be *investing* or *driving*? Let's first take a look at the different pathways for engaging in learning, as they will be the focus for setting intentions for engagement. Then, we will turn our attention to the different paths that students might take when disengaging, as this will be an important part of monitoring engagement during learning.

PATHWAYS OF ENGAGING	
***Participating* Pathway**	I am listening, paying attention, following instructions, answering the teacher's questions, staying on task, asking questions if I'm not sure what to do, and completing the activities assigned by the teacher.

(Continued)

(Continued)

PATHWAYS OF ENGAGING	
***Investing* Pathway**	I am asking questions when I get confused about what we are learning, asking for help if I need it, sharing my ideas and opinions with others, thinking of interesting questions to investigate, explaining why learning this is important to me, and trying things even if I'm not sure they will work.
***Driving* Pathway**	I am setting goals for myself, making a plan to achieve my goals, asking others for feedback to help me improve, looking for challenges to take on, checking in on my progress along the way, reflecting on my mistakes, thinking about how to improve, collaborating with others on a shared goal, and challenging others to help them make progress and improve.

While it is true that we are aiming to empower all students to choose *driving* and be successful in driving their learning, we need to allow for different pathways. Not all students will be ready to jump straight into *driving*, *driving* may not be possible for every lesson and topic, and learning experiences may not require *driving* all the time. Take the experience of reading this book, for example. Given you are reading it now, you are at least on the pathway of *participating*—reading what has been written and reflecting when prompted. Some may choose to stop at this level, but others will find their interest and curiosity growing as they make their way through the chapters. Hopefully, some of you are already *investing* in the things you are reading about—having questions about what you are reading, seeing the value in the ideas for you and your students, or wanting to discuss what you are thinking with others. Although there may be exceptions, for most people it is probably still too early to shift into *driving* mode—setting goals and making plans for how you will apply the ideas, taking action to establish a partnership for engagement with your students, actively striving to improve your autonomy-supportive practices, or collaborating with colleagues to move forward together. As you read through the book, see if you can detect changes to your engagement and identify what it is that prompted the shift. The more we are in tune with our inner motivations and engagement choices, the better equipped we will be to support our students to do the same.

These pathways for engagement are also a useful reference point for teachers when we are planning. If we expect to empower students to move from *participating* to *driving*, then we need to make sure that the activities and lessons we plan enable increasing levels of challenge and agency, rather than constraining students to the *participating* pathway. Likewise, if we only plan for the *driving* pathway without any option for students to begin with *participating* or *investing*, then students may get frustrated or discouraged if they are not quite ready for the challenge of *driving*.

Once students understand the different engagement pathways, they can collaborate with you to develop success criteria for their engagement that are specific to the learning intention and planned activities. These criteria will describe what successful engagement looks like at different levels, allowing students to monitor what path they are on and have a clear idea about what the next level of engagement will involve. We will continue to look at these pathways of engaging in Chapter 4.

While it does not make sense to encourage students to set an intention to disengage from the learning experience, we need to consider the potential barriers to engagement that might send a student down a pathway of disengaging. Knowing the reasons why students might disengage, as well as the signs that a student is disengaging, will help us to plan for preventing disengagement and responding to it if it does happen. We will look at the different pathways of disengaging next.

CHECKING IN ON ENGAGEMENT

As a teacher, you are probably used to monitoring student engagement during a lesson. This is one of the first things we learn when we start teaching, as disengagement can go hand in hand with having your plans for teaching and learning suddenly run off the rails. We soon learn that keeping an eye out for the signs of disengagement is a necessary part of managing the classroom. Perhaps it is not surprising that some teachers get stuck thinking about engagement as an aspect of classroom management but not thinking about it as an aspect of learning. This type of thinking may help us to keep the classroom running smoothly with minimal disruptions, but that does not mean that students are learning and making progress. Just because students are busy, productive, attentive, and able to give the right answers does not mean they are learning. Likewise, a calm orderly classroom where the curriculum is covered, explanations are given, and feedback is supplied does not equate to learning. Rob Coe (2015) identifies these things as "poor proxies for learning" and warns against using them as evidence that learning is occurring. While it is important to maintain an environment that limits disruptions to teaching and learning, we need to do more than monitor behavior and productivity. If we want to make sure that students are learning, we need to monitor their thinking and ensure the tasks we design make them think hard enough to make a difference to what they know and what they can do.

TIME TO REFLECT

How do you monitor engagement?

What signs do you look for that the student is disengaged from learning?

What signs do you look for that the student is engaged in learning?

Have you ever fallen into the trap of assuming that students who stay on task and get their work done are learning?

Have you ever had an experience with a student whom you considered to be engaged but who had not demonstrated any growth in understanding or skills?

Thinking of your own experiences as a student, did you ever feel like you were doing what was asked of you but not learning anything new?

We might have well-developed strategies for monitoring engagement during lessons, but we are only one side of the engagement partnership. Involving students in monitoring their engagement is an important part of the process. Asking students to check in on their engagement during learning and seeking feedback from students on their engagement are some of the ways we can support students to contribute to the process. Having them check in on their progress in learning at the same time as they are checking in on their level of engagement will mean they are thinking about what actions they have been taking to help them learn *and* what progress they have made with the learning intention and success criteria. In this way, we are explicitly linking their engagement with their progress and learning, and supporting them to feel that both are within their control.

The pathways of engaging can support students as they reflect on their engagement and look for evidence to evaluate their current level of engagement. For example, "I think I'm on the *investing* pathway because I asked you a question when I got confused about the example they showed in the video, and I was sharing my ideas with the group for how we might solve the problem." But what happens if the student is on a pathway of disengagement? To better support students to reflect on and evaluate their engagement, we need to describe all of the different pathways that students might find themselves on while checking in.

LOOKING FOR EVIDENCE OF DISENGAGEMENT

When checking in on engagement, one of the things we are looking for is any sign that the student is disengaged. Expert teachers are amazing in their ability to pick up subtle cues from individual students that tell them the student is on a path of disengaging from learning.

SNAPSHOT OF PRACTICE

In one lesson I was observing, the students were working in groups to solve problems involving fractions. As the teacher was working with one group, I saw her look over at another group and suggest they use a times table chart to help them with the task. One of the girls got up, went to her desk to retrieve the chart, and went back to the group and started working. The teacher continued working with her focus group. Later, when we were discussing the interaction, the teacher elaborated.

"When I looked over, I saw that she was not engaged in the task. She was sitting back from the other two, mumbling to herself and pulling at her hair—I know her; those are the signs she is finding it too difficult. She has come a long way in math this year, but she is still struggling with confidence, and if I let it go too long, she will just shut down and refuse

(Continued)

(Continued)

> *to do anything. I suppose it's that connection that you have with them and the relationship that you form. I think that's the key; if you know what they're like, you let certain things go, and you don't let certain things go. You push them where they need to be pushed; you give them more support where they need it. But you have to know each kid to know what's relevant, and so you have to take an active interest, I think—that's the key."*

Both teacher and student contribute their insights to the checking-in process, and this is especially important when it comes to disengagement. The aim is to understand where students are at and try to see things from their perspective, not to punish, shame, or coerce them into behaving, feeling, or thinking the way that we want. Ultimately, we want to work together, as partners, to plan a path that will help them to engage rather than disengage from learning. We will take a closer look at how we can prevent and respond to student disengagement from learning in Chapter 5, but for now, let's look at the different pathways of disengaging.

As we did with the pathways of engaging, we can support students to identify their own disengagement by establishing an agreed-upon set of behaviors that are indicative of each form of disengaging. We can start with the general behaviors from the continuum (Chapter 1), but also work with the students to describe these pathways in a way that makes sense to the students and relates to the learning context and environment. Getting students' input in describing the different forms of engagement and disengagement is one way we can show that we value their perspective, but it also helps them to connect the six forms of engagement with their previous experiences of learning. The better they understand the different pathways of engaging and disengaging, the more useful they will be in the checking-in process.

PATHWAYS OF DISENGAGING	
***Withdrawing* Pathway**	I am distracted, thinking about other things, trying to go unnoticed by others, sitting away from others in my group or at the back of the room, trying to get by with minimal effort, watching the clock, and drawing to pass the time, and I don't care about what we are doing.

PATHWAYS OF DISENGAGING	
Avoiding **Pathway**	I am looking for ways to avoid doing the work, looking for reasons to leave the room or move around the room, not prepared with the things I need to get to work, doing other things rather than the work, playing around with others or with materials, and talking with others about things that don't relate to what we are learning.
Disrupting **Pathway**	I am looking for ways to disrupt the lesson or disrupt other students who are working, refusing to participate or work, arguing with the teacher or with other people in the class, and trying to distract others from their work.

WHERE TO NEXT FOR ENGAGEMENT?

Being able to identify the engagement pathway a student is on is one thing, but to prepare us for the final step in the process we may need a little more information—particularly if the student is on a pathway of disengaging. Getting to the bottom of why students have chosen not to invest their effort and motivation into learning is a necessary part of deciding what to do next. We may have some ideas about what is happening, particularly if we know a student well, but we need to check in with the student to know for sure. Asking students to provide feedback on their engagement can help us to figure out how to help them want to choose a pathway of engaging, and it helps them to become aware of and take responsibility for their engagement in learning. In Chapter 5, we will look at the common causes of disengagement and strategies for preventing or responding to disengagement.

Identifying the next steps for engagement is best done in tandem with identifying the "Where to next?" for learning so that students can marry up the next target for learning with an intention for how they are going to take actions that will put them on an engagement path for achieving that target. The next steps will depend on the students and where they are at in their learning and engagement, but the aim is to support students to choose engaging over disengaging and move along the continuum from *participating* to *driving*. As with every other step in the process, this is done in collaboration with the student, to identify what the teacher can do and what the student can do to improve engagement and learning. Things that teachers can do (in consultation with students) include making adjustments to the task or the learning environment in response to feedback from students, supporting students to identify what they think might be the next steps they could take, and encouraging students to stretch themselves and take on increasing challenges. We will look at this in more detail in the coming chapters.

WHAT CAN TEACHERS DO?

Redefine the rules of engagement . . . and have patience in the face of resistance. Students might need help to unlearn certain patterns of engagement as the rules of the game change. If students have come to understand that being a student at school means getting tasks done, getting answers correct, and doing things quickly, then we may need to shift the narrative to one of progress-making, challenge-seeking, collaborating, and taking action—helping them to think like a learner. Some students may have developed certain engagement patterns that will have to be unlearned if they want to succeed in mastering their engagement. For example, some high-achieving students may be used to winning at the old game of school—that is, doing what the teacher asks, getting things right, getting things done, and getting things in on time. These students are not used to making mistakes or failing and may resist any attempt to change the rules. For these students, the new rules may require more effort, more inner motivation, and more risk. Other students might have a pattern of withdrawing and trying to fly under the radar. Now that we are changing the rules, it becomes harder to do that because we are asking them to set intentions for engaging, discuss the specific behaviors they will engage in as they try to make progress, and evaluate their engagement during learning—holding everyone (teachers and students) accountable for engagement through the process described in this chapter. As you work with students to redefine the rules of engagement, acknowledge and respect that this might be very challenging and uncomfortable for some. It may be challenging and uncomfortable for you too! Keep the lines of communication open, be open about your own struggles with the new rules, and look for ways to collaboratively move forward together.

Teach students the language and process for engagement. All students will benefit from your support as you help them to become aware of their engagement patterns, start to use the new language and process for engagement, and develop the skills and confidence needed to take ownership of their engagement in learning. Allow time to introduce the different forms of engagement from the continuum, and provide multiple opportunities for students to use the language and develop a common understanding of what each of these forms means. Remember, the goal is to turn this process into a habit as we teach students to think like a learner.

Take the students' perspective and seek their input. When introducing the engagement continuum, we want students to connect it to their own experiences of learning. Rather than just telling students, "This is what it means to be *withdrawing* or *investing*" and then moving on, we want to hear their insights and experiences of trying to withdraw from a learning experience or feeling very invested in learning something. We want to know what it feels like, what they do and what they don't do, and how they are thinking. Together we can build a rich picture of each form of engagement and a meaningful vocabulary for discussing engagement. Seeking the input of students during this initial stage of introducing the continuum also sets the tone for our new engagement partnership where students are required to actively participate in the process and share the responsibility for engagement in learning.

Gather evidence and challenge your assumptions. When asking students to evaluate their engagement, we ask them to back up their claims with evidence. We need to do the same when we are evaluating student engagement or making assumptions about engagement and learning in our class. We may think we know when our students are engaging and when they are disengaging, but that is not always the case. This is especially true when it comes to the passive forms of *withdrawing* and *participating*, which can look very similar. Many students who are very adept at flying under the radar are also quite successful at school. These students are able to go unnoticed because they have perfected the art of putting in minimal effort while still completing tasks and achieving (but not necessarily learning). Rather than assume we know what is going on, we must look for ways of gathering evidence to test those assumptions. Ideally, we work with others (colleagues and students) to gather this evidence to make sure that our own biases are not getting in the way of seeing what is really happening.

CHAPTER 4

Let's Get Engaged!

"The kids were just so surprised. I was surprised at their surprise in realizing, 'Oh, it's not my teacher's job to engage me. I have to be an active participant. My teacher and I are in partnership in this learning process.' They had not considered that before. It has been fascinating to watch that process of goal setting each day—'How am I going to be engaged?'—and then check back in with them to see, 'How have you done? And what will you do better tomorrow so that you can be a better learner and get a little more progress?'"

—Middle school teacher on using the continuum
to set intentions for engagement

Recently, I was having a conversation with a group of teachers about their use of the continuum of engagement. One of the teachers remarked, "Sometimes I will have a lesson where it's just about *participating*. I'll have to say to the students, 'Today's lesson is not a *driving* lesson.'" This comment sparked a discussion about the nature of engagement and how it fluctuates within a lesson. Sometimes this is by design, for example when we move from demonstrating or explaining something to an activity where the students will apply this in some way. Sometimes engagement just fluctuates naturally, moving between periods of active engagement and periods of more passive engagement. You might even notice this yourself as you are reading this book. You might have periods where you are actively thinking about what you are reading, connecting it with your experiences in the classroom, or finding yourself wondering about how you might implement the ideas with your students. However, you might also have times when you are distracted, tired, or just having trouble getting into what you are reading. This is natural. Teaching our students to recognize these natural patterns and fluctuations in engagement is an important part of developing their skills in mastering their engagement. Rather than thinking of the engagement pathways as separate roads to stay on for the whole lesson or activity, it might be more useful to think of them as adjacent lanes on a highway. This allows us to think about and discuss the movement from lane to lane at different points during learning. At times, a student might begin in the *participating* lane but change to the *investing* or *driving* lane and stay there for most of the activity. At other times, students might be mostly in the *participating* lane but have periods sitting in the *investing* or *driving* lane. Even in situations where *participating* will be the dominant pathway for engaging, there are still opportunities for students to apply *investing* and *driving* behaviors.

In this chapter, we will look more deeply into each of the three engagement pathways. The goal is for students to choose a pathway of engaging rather than a pathway of disengaging from learning, but that does not mean that we expect them to be *driving* all the time. That is neither sustainable nor sensible. In the engagement partnership, sometimes teachers will take the lead (e.g., when explaining a new concept), and other times students will take the lead (e.g., when discussing a plan for solving a problem during a collaborative task). When students have a deep understanding of the different pathways for engaging in learning and a level of skill at implementing the behaviors associated with each different pathway, they will be equipped to actively manage their engagement in learning. As teachers, we can help them by doing each of the following:

- Ensuring our students can successfully *participate*, *invest*, and *drive* their learning forward
- Providing opportunities to identify, apply, and practice *participating*, *investing*, and *driving* behaviors
- Working with students to cultivate the inner motivational resources that will fuel their motivation to *participate*, *invest*, and *drive* during learning

Ideally, we are aiming for students to be able to select a pathway for engaging in learning and justify that pathway based on the intentions for learning and the learning activity they will be engaging in, as well as their own internal motivational resources and needs. This will take practice, like any new skill, but we now have a rich language and an embedded process to support this skill development.

LET'S GET *PARTICIPATING!*

When students are engaged at the *participating* level, they are prepared to invest enough motivation and effort to follow the directions and instructions of the teacher (or peers). This is the most passive form of engagement, but it is still a step toward learning rather than away from it. This will probably be the most familiar form of engagement for students, as it involves behaviors associated with the traditional rules of engagement at school. It may come as quite a shock to some students that there is more to engaging than just *participating*, as one middle school teacher recently shared with me:

"The way that the behaviors are laid out on the continuum, and described to show what that looks like . . . sometimes kids are uncomfortable because they realize that, 'Oh, I'm participating but I'm not really investing; I'm not really driving.' And that changes things for them because they realize that they have to ramp it up. Helping to pull that out for them is very impactful, I think."

WHAT DOES PARTICIPATING LOOK LIKE?

Essentially, the indicators of *participating* revolve around students doing what the teacher (or a peer in the case of a group task) has told them to do. It is passive in the sense that the students are acting with limited autonomy or agency even though they may be busy "doing" something and not just listening and watching others. It would be incorrect to think that *participating* is undesirable or something to be avoided. After all, it is better to participate in the learning activity than to choose not to participate. But more importantly, there are behaviors on the *participating* pathway that can be very helpful for both learning and motivation to engage in that learning. For example, paying attention while someone explains how to use a new strategy and listening carefully to the instructions for an activity are important. Doing these things helps students to know what to do and how to do it, meaning they are in a better position to engage with the activity rather than disengage because they are not sure what to do. When students are unsure of what to do, choosing to ask for help or clarify an instruction is also an example of a *participating* behavior that can be productive for learning and engagement. This is preferable to students sitting back and waiting for someone to notice they need help. Finally, being able to ignore distractions and remain focused on the task at hand is a desirable behavior for learning if the task is sufficiently challenging to support improvement in skills or understanding—that is, if the task is not something students can already accomplish easily and they are likely to make some progress in their learning through the process of completing the task.

KEY MESSAGE

The benefits of the *participating* pathway will depend on the potential for the pathway to contribute to motivation and/or learning. When choosing this pathway, both teachers and students need to identify and explain how *participating* right now might benefit learning and support the students' motivation to take their engagement to the next level.

Participating by Design: What Might the Teacher Be Planning for at This Level?

"I want the students to follow my lead and complete certain tasks."

When planning, teachers who are aiming for students to be at the *participating* level will be focused on taking the lead in learning and having the students follow their lead. This may be the entry point for engaging in certain situations, for example when students are less confident in what they know or what they can do. At certain points in the teaching and learning process, we may want to take the lead as we support students to build certain foundational skills or knowledge—for example, when we want to model a new strategy, introduce a new topic, or address a misconception that has emerged. But, ultimately our goal is to have students move beyond *participating* rather than stay at that level of engagement. When we plan activities or periods of the lesson where students will primarily be on the *participating* pathway, it is important to explain why and also look for opportunities for students to engage in *investing* and *driving* behaviors to support those who are ready to move beyond *participating*. We will look at this in more detail later in the chapter.

SETTING INTENTIONS FOR PARTICIPATING: WHAT INTENTIONS FOR ENGAGEMENT MIGHT THE STUDENT SET AT THIS LEVEL?

"I want someone else to take the lead, and I will follow."

When setting intentions for engagement at the *participating* level, students can select specific behaviors from the *participating* pathway to learning. These behaviors help students plan for how they will engage in learning and provide a reference point for monitoring engagement during learning. In Chapter 3, we looked at some common behaviors that sit on this pathway of engaging. These include the following:

I will listen and pay attention.

I will follow instructions.

I will answer the teacher's questions.

I will stay on task.

I will ask questions if I am not sure what to do.

I will finish the activities assigned by the teacher.

These are general *participating* behaviors, but ideally, you will work with your students to describe the *participating* pathway that is relevant to the learning activity in a language that makes sense to you and your students. This is true of each of the engagement pathways.

WHY MIGHT A STUDENT CHOOSE THE PARTICIPATING PATHWAY?

Some students might prefer to build their confidence before taking on the added challenge associated with *investing* and *driving*. For example, they might choose to work through some practice problems and check their answers before applying those skills to a more open-ended investigation. Or, they might choose to work with the teacher in a focus group to get a better understanding of a new concept or strategy before they tackle an independent or group task that builds on this foundational knowledge.

SNAPSHOT OF PRACTICE

It's not uncommon for teachers to work with small groups of students during a lesson to provide extra support or scaffolding. Unfortunately, rather than teachers supporting student autonomy and having them opt into these groups, students are often conscripted into the teacher group based on ability level. It does not take students long to work out that they are always in the "low" group (or "dumb" group as one of my second graders once told me). Rather than aiding motivation and learning, this approach can have devastating and long-term effects on student engagement at school. There are ways of providing

(Continued)

(Continued)

extra support and supporting student autonomy and competence at the same time.

One of the teachers I observed used opt-in support sessions she called "clinics" to provide extra scaffolding or support when needed. She made a habit of letting groups or individuals get started on the task and used that time to quickly check in with those she thought might need a bit of help getting going. At the same time, she was looking for specific areas of need across the class. She would then announce that she was going to run a short clinic focusing on whatever need she had identified. The students could determine for themselves if this was something they wanted help with. Students were free to leave the clinic at any point if they felt confident enough to go back to the task. Over the several lessons I observed, it was clear that there was no stigma in attending a clinic, and it was not always the same students each time. According to the teacher, it took a little while for students to get used to the process and make use of it to support their learning. Now that it is familiar, students sometimes proactively request a clinic when they get stuck on something and need help.

WHAT DO STUDENTS NEED TO PARTICIPATE?

To be able to *participate* in the learning activity, students need to know what to do, how to do it, and how to get help if they need it. Without this, it will be difficult for them to find their way onto the *participating* pathway.

Staying on the *participating* pathway also requires students to be able to ignore distractions and remain focused, and show that they care enough to invest their effort and motivation in engaging in participating behaviors.

LET'S GET **INVESTED!**

When students are *investing* in their learning, they are interested enough and motivated enough to take a more active role in learning. The move from *participating* to *investing* may well be a bigger step to take than moving from *investing* to *driving* because it requires students to move beyond the familiar old rules of engagement that only require passive compliance. *Investing* requires a level of commitment to getting interested, being curious, and finding the value in learning—not just relying on someone else to make it interesting or relevant. This is where the engagement partnership really starts to take off as students begin to actively contribute to the process. In one high school class, the teacher introduced the students to the continuum, and the class discussed the different forms of engagement. The teacher was impressed with the depth of the students' thinking and the insights they shared during the discussion. Many commented that they had no idea engagement had so many different aspects to it, suggesting their thinking had moved from a surface-level understanding to something deeper. One comment, in particular, stood out to the teacher because it showed a growing appreciation of engagement as a choice made by the student:

"I've never really thought about this before, but boredom is a choice."

—High school student

WHAT DOES INVESTING LOOK LIKE?

When students are *investing*, they are showing signs that they want to learn more, understand better, or become more skilled. This desire may be driven by feelings of being interested in or curious about what is being learned. Or, it may be that the outcome of learning is believed to be personally valuable in some way. For example, learning about the road rules in preparation for a driving test is probably not inherently interesting for most people, but the prospect of getting a license makes it worth investing the effort needed to learn those rules. Many of the things associated with *investing* have the potential to energize motivation and accelerate learning, including being curious, enjoying learning, perceiving the learning activity to be meaningful or valuable, acting with a sense of agency, and connecting with others during learning. In addition, students who are *investing* take proactive steps to further their learning by identifying the gaps in their knowledge or understanding, sharing their thinking and questions with others, asking others to share their thinking, and taking risks in pursuit of improvement.

There are important distinctions between help-seeking at the *participating* level and help-seeking at the *investing* level. At the *participating* level, students ask questions about the task or activity (e.g., What do I have to do? How do I do it? Is this correct?), and they seek help that supports them to complete the assigned task or activity. The focus is on getting a task done. At the *investing* level, students ask questions about the concept or learning focus (e.g., How is that different from . . . ? Why did . . . ? What would happen if . . . ?), and they seek help that supports them to improve their understanding or skill. The focus is on learning and improving.

Investing by Design: What Might the Teacher Be Planning for at This Level?

"I want the students to be interested in learning and actively involved in the process."

When planning for students to become *invested* in their learning, we are intending for them to move beyond following our lead and take a more active role in learning. As a start, we need to make sure that the learning activity enables them to become actively *invested* and limits the possibility that they can remain in passive *participating* mode. When planning for ways that students can move on from *participating* activities, we are looking for something that requires more thinking, enables the students to become interested or curious, and has the potential to be more meaningful or valuable to the students.

KEY MESSAGE

Investing is not about doing more hands-on, practical activities (although this might be involved); it is about doing more thinking. When learning is the goal, becoming more actively engaged needs to involve increasing the level of minds-on activity, not just increasing busyness. We want students to move from *participating* to *investing* not simply because they will be more active, but because that activity has the potential to accelerate their learning and progress.

Planning for *investing* does not have to involve a complete change to everything we do. Sometimes this can be done with a simple adjustment or addition to an otherwise passive learning activity. For example:

PARTICIPATING	INVESTING
• Look up a list of vocabulary words and write down the definitions. • Listen to the teacher explain the new vocabulary words. Write them down in your notebook.	• Skim the text before reading and make a list of words you are not familiar with or you are unsure about. If you think you might know what it means, write your guess next to the word.

PARTICIPATING	INVESTING
• Complete a worksheet focusing on the vocabulary words (e.g., a crossword or matching the word with the definition).	• Come up with a visual way of showing what the word means and share it with a partner (e.g., a picture or symbol). • Working with a partner, investigate the possible connections between these words. How might you classify and group these words based on these connections?

If you are introducing a new strategy or process, such as concept mapping or skimming a text, you will need to teach it first and give the students multiple opportunities to practice using the strategy. Ultimately, we aim to get to the stage where the strategy becomes an established method for taking engagement from passive *participating* to active *investing*. Make this explicit to students by telling them that the activity is designed to help them move from the *participating* pathway to the *investing* pathway. This will help them to make the distinction between the types of things they do when *participating* and the types of things they do when *investing*. Remember, the rules of engagement and the process of engaging should be understood by all, not just the teacher.

HELPING STUDENTS TAKE RESPONSIBILITY FOR GETTING INVESTED

Designing learning activities that enable students to move beyond *participating* is important, but students still need to find the inner motivation to get *invested* in learning. Moving from *participating* to *investing* requires students to put in more effort, and this relies on their motivation to want to learn. Students may be surprised to find out that they are expected to take responsibility for getting interested and finding the personal value or meaningful connection to their lives. The message we want to get across is that we are there to support students to move from *participating* to *investing*, but they have to make the choice to become *invested*.

What happens when a student refuses to move beyond *participating*? One high school teacher shared his experiences of using the engagement continuum with his students and the many positive benefits he had observed for his students. Students were using the continuum to set intentions for their engagement and to reflect on their engagement later on. While many students expressed the benefits of getting into *driving* mode, one student explicitly refused to move beyond *participating*. This high-achieving student simply stated, "I am never going to do any more than *participate*. I am here to get my score. I know I could do all that, but I've got other stuff to worry about." A good example of a student who has excelled at the old game of engagement and is actively resisting any change to the rules, this student was acting with agency and choosing a strategic path, one that had proven successful in the past.

While we cannot force students to set intentions beyond *participating*, that does not mean we cannot do our part to encourage them to become more engaged. For one thing, we can evaluate the learning activities that we set for students to make sure that students need to move beyond *participating* if they want to achieve higher levels of success (acknowledging this is not always possible in terms of some standardized assessment tasks). We still need to allow for students to be on the *participating* pathway when this is what is needed, but we also need to raise the bar where possible for students to understand that if they expect to make more progress in their learning, then they also need to expect to put more effort in.

Beyond that, we can work with students to help them identify the times when they are engaging in *investing* or *driving* behaviors during learning, even if they have not set an intention to be engaged at those levels. This might start with us actively looking for evidence of these behaviors, feeding that back to the student, and then asking them to explain why they chose to act in that way at that moment. Rather than persist with a battle over whether students will raise their intentions for engagement, this approach seeks to engage them in conversations about their engagement choices during learning activities.

STRATEGIES TO SUPPORT INVESTING

Sometimes we are faced with something that is not immediately interesting or meaningful, making it hard to get motivated to invest much effort into learning it. How can teachers help students manage and build their motivation to learn? Of course, it is not as simple as telling students to get more interested or care more about learning, but we can help them to develop strategies for finding their interests and making connections that are meaningful to them. Strategies or routines that help us to think about something in a different way can be a useful approach to getting *invested* in what we are learning. These include strategies for all of the following:

- Thinking creatively or flexibly
- Thinking more deeply
- Developing curiosity and generating interesting questions
- Making meaningful connections
- Thinking with others

The Project Zero (n.d.) team at Harvard has been researching the use of learning routines to support student thinking for many years. They have developed an extensive collection of resources and thinking routines that are freely available online (www.pz.harvard.edu/thinking-routines). This resource is a great place to start when looking for strategies to support students to transition from *participating* to getting *invested* in learning. As students become more familiar with and skilled at using the strategies, they will be in a position to select strategies they think will be useful in getting themselves *invested* in learning—for example, using a *Think, Puzzle, Explore* routine to tap into their curiosity about a new topic or using the *Step in–Step out–Step back* routine to help them think about a historical event from different perspectives.

SETTING INTENTIONS FOR INVESTING: WHAT INTENTIONS FOR ENGAGEMENT MIGHT THE STUDENT SET AT THIS LEVEL?

"I want to be interested in learning, to be actively involved in the process of learning, and to interact with others to help me engage and learn."

Essentially, being *invested* means students are finding the learning personally interesting or valuable enough to want to think more deeply about it and find out more. General behaviors from the *investing* pathway that students might refer to as they set their intentions for engagement include the following:

I will ask questions to improve my understanding.

I will ask someone for help if I need it.

I will share my ideas and opinions with others.

I will think of interesting questions to investigate or discuss.

I will try things even if I'm not sure they will work.

I will look for connections between what we are learning and things I find interesting or important.

I will explain why learning this is important to me.

Where possible, work with the students to customize these actions on the *investing* pathway so they make sense for the learning activity and context for learning.

WHAT SKILLS DO STUDENTS NEED TO GET INVESTED?

At the *investing* level, students are becoming more active contributors to the engagement partnership. They are moving away from following someone else's lead and beginning to make decisions and take actions to further their engagement and learning. To get *invested*, students need to be able to identify what they know and can do and what they want to know or be able to do. That is, they need to be able to find their reason for wanting to invest more effort and motivation into learning. Sometimes the learning activity is inherently interesting and has obvious personal value to a student, making this move to *investing* easier. When that is not the case, students can be supported to use different strategies for finding the interest or value in what they are learning, such as the strategies we looked at earlier.

LET'S GET DRIVING!

At the *driving* level of engagement, students are actively thinking about their learning, have clear goals in mind about where they want to get to and why, and have a plan for how they will get there. The inner motivational resources that provided the foundation for students to want to become *invested* in learning are now strong enough to fuel the shift into *driving* mode. Motivation alone is not sufficient; students also need to have the opportunity to take on a learning challenge that allows them to *drive* and the right skills to enable them to *drive* their learning successfully forward.

WHAT DOES DRIVING LOOK LIKE?

When students are *driving*, they know what they want to achieve, and they are proactively making moves designed to help them move forward in that direction. They set goals or targets for themselves and make decisions about how they will work toward these targets, take actions that support their progress, and monitor how they are tracking along the way. According to Visible Learning Meta[x] (2021), many of the key behaviors associated with *driving* have the potential to accelerate or considerably accelerate student achievement, including engaging in self-directed learning, self-evaluation, self-reflection, accessing feedback, and being deeply motivated and committed to a goal (www.visiblelearningmetax .com/influences). A key aspect of *driving* is the proactive interaction with others as a strategy to support learning. This can involve actions such as seeking feedback, engaging in discussions or debates that challenge and take thinking to a deeper level, planning together, reflecting together, and teaching each other. We will have a closer look at the important role of peers in engagement and how students might take on the challenge of *driving* together in Chapter 6.

Driving by Design: What Might the Teacher Be Planning for at This Level?

"I want the students to be proactive and collaborative learners."

If we want students to take the *driving* pathway, then we need to design learning experiences that not only enable those behaviors but require them. Because *driving* often involves a certain amount of iteration as students seek and respond to feedback to make improvements, it can take time. Tasks that have students working over an extended period or across several lessons are ideally suited to *driving*. Let's have a look at some examples of activities that might sit on different engagement pathways for learning to help us get a sense of how the challenge and level of active engagement increases as the student moves from *participating* to *driving*.

PARTICIPATING PATHWAY	INVESTING PATHWAY	DRIVING PATHWAY
Answer a set of questions about a narrative text. Questions involve recalling events from the story, making inferences about the feelings or motivations of characters, and questions about the choices or strategies the author used to tell the story.	Work with a partner to think of three changes you could make to that story that you think would be interesting. Explain each change and why it might be interesting for a reader. Share your ideas with another pair of students and ask them to rank your ideas from most interesting to least interesting.	Working in a group of three, innovate on the text and create a new story for a particular audience. You decide who the audience is, how you will change the story, and what format the story will be presented in. Buddy up with another group to act as feedback partners as you create your new story.

SETTING INTENTIONS FOR DRIVING: WHAT INTENTIONS FOR ENGAGEMENT MIGHT THE STUDENT SET AT THIS LEVEL?

When students are setting an intention to be on the *driving* pathway, they might consider the following actions:

> *I will set goals for what I want to achieve.*
>
> *I will make a plan to achieve those goals.*
>
> *I will ask others for feedback to help me improve.*
>
> *I will look for challenges that might help me learn more.*
>
> *I will check in on my progress and engagement along the way.*
>
> *I will reflect on my mistakes and learn from them.*
>
> *I will look for ways to improve.*
>
> *I will collaborate with others to achieve a shared goal.*

Asking students to come up with their own list of *driving* actions they intend to implement to take their learning forward is another way of empowering them to take this pathway.

WHAT SKILLS DO STUDENTS NEED TO GET DRIVING?

At the *driving* level, students are at their most active. They are proactively taking actions to support their engagement and learning. To successfully *drive* their learning forward, students need to be able to identify where they want to get to and how they plan to get there. They also need strategies and tools to help them reflect on their learning and engagement and evaluate their progress along the way. Having clear learning intentions and success criteria in place and establishing a regular process for checking in on engagement and learning can support students with these aspects of *driving*. An important part of *driving* is connecting with others to energize motivation and take thinking and learning to a deeper level.

CHECKING IN ON ENGAGEMENT

When checking in on engagement, we are referring back to the original intentions for engagement and considering any adjustments that might be made to achieve those intentions or potentially raise those intentions. One of the things we are looking out for is evidence that students may have drifted onto a path of disengaging. When this is the case, we need to work with the students to help them get back on track for engaging, something we will look at more closely in the next chapter. The other thing we are looking for is evidence that might indicate that students are ready to move to a different engagement pathway. This might involve moving to a more active form of engagement, for example moving from *participating* to *investing*. Or, it could involve stepping to a lower level of engagement to access additional support, for example moving into a teacher-led small group to work through an area of confusion or misunderstanding.

KEY MESSAGE: ARE THEY ENGAGING OR DISENGAGING?

Both *participating* and *withdrawing* are passive forms of engagement. As such, they can look similar on the surface. For example, students can appear to be looking at you, listening to you, or focusing on their work when really they have drifted onto the *withdrawing* pathway and are mentally checked out. If the task is too easy and does not require a lot of effort, it is also possible that students can get it done while operating at the *withdrawing* level of engagement. Much like being on autopilot when we are driving, the task gets done, but the mind is thinking about other things during the process with limited learning taking place.

Similarly, students might appear to be distracted and not listening when in reality they are listening and thinking about what you are saying, just not looking very compliant. When I was teaching kindergarten, I had a student who regularly hopped around like a frog during mat time but also managed to stop and share very insightful comments that showed he was listening and mentally engaged. Of course, as students get older, this is often more subtle. For example, staring out of a window while thinking about what they are learning can look very similar to staring out the window and daydreaming about what they are going to do on the weekend.

When in doubt about what you are seeing or hearing, look for more evidence to help you make sense of what is going on. Asking the students to check in on their engagement will provide additional information about where they are at and what might need to happen next.

CHECKING IN AS A TEACHER

When checking in on students' engagement during learning, several questions can guide us:

- Is there evidence of the students engaging in *participating* behaviors? *Investing* behaviors? *Driving* behaviors?
- What engagement pathway did the students intend to be on? Are they on it?
- Is there evidence the students are engaging in *withdrawing, avoiding,* or *disrupting* behaviors?
- Is there evidence the students may be ready to move to the *investing* or *driving* pathway?

CHECKING IN AS A STUDENT

When students are asked to check in on their engagement, there are similar questions that can guide their reflection:

- What engagement pathway did I intend to be on? What pathway have I been on, and what evidence do I have that I have been on that pathway?
- Am I ready to move to the *investing* or *driving* pathway? Do I need any help to do that?
- Is there evidence I have been engaging in *withdrawing, avoiding,* or *disrupting* behaviors? What can I do to get onto an engagement pathway? What help do I need?

WHERE TO NEXT?

The information that we gather during checking in will provide some indication of the next steps for engagement. For example, if students have found themselves on a path of disengaging, then the focus will be on working with them to identify what steps both students and teacher can take to support them to get back on a pathway of engaging. We will look at this in more detail in the next chapter.

If a student and the teacher decide it is time to step up to *investing* or *driving,* then the focus will be on identifying the specific behaviors or actions that will support this. This includes actions the teacher will take to support the student in this move, as well as actions the student will take to ramp up the engagement (see Figure 4.1).

FIGURE 4.1 ● The Engagement Pathways at a Glance

	PARTICIPATING PATHWAY	INVESTING PATHWAY	DRIVING PATHWAY
What is the role of teacher and student?	The teacher takes the lead and makes the decisions about learning. The student follows. Student is passive.	The teacher encourages input from the student. The student contributes ideas, questions, interests, and preferences for learning. Student contributes their voice to decisions about learning.	The teacher sets the context for learning and supports the student to reach their goal. The student takes the lead and sets a goal for learning. Student is acting with agency to take their learning forward.
Planning for this pathway	Activities are often closed, highly structured, and constrained to one lesson. Focus is on getting it correct.	Activities involve opportunities for dialogue and encourage critical and creative thinking, curiosity, questions, and meaningful connections. Focus is on thinking more deeply.	Activities are more open-ended, less structured, and optimally challenging; provide opportunities for feedback and reflection; and spread over a more extended period of time. Focus is on improving.
What are the preconditions for engaging?	Requires a willingness to comply and a level of confidence in their ability to succeed in the task.	Requires a level of interest or value in learning more and the confidence to have a voice in their learning.	Requires a willingness to embrace challenges, strategies to support improvement, and the ability to persist in the face of setbacks.
What does it look like?	Paying attention, responding to teacher questions, staying on task, getting work done, and asking questions that clarify instructions and expectations.	Asking questions that take thinking deeper, being curious, sharing ideas, making connections during learning, showing an interest in learning more, and explaining the value in learning.	Setting goals for learning, making a plan for learning, collaborating with others to learn, seeking feedback to improve, reflecting on learning, and evaluating progress.

TIME TO REFLECT

Before we move on to tackle the different forms of disengaging, take some time to reflect on your current engagement practices to get a sense of where you and your students are at. As a start, we want to identify the things that are in place and working well, as these things can serve as a foundation on which to build. These questions might help you to reflect on your current practices:

- When planning, do I design activities for all three engagement pathways? Do I give equal attention to different pathways of engaging, or do I tend to focus on just one or two pathways?
- What strategies/activities do I currently use to support *participating*? *Investing*? *Driving*?
- Are my students familiar with using learning intentions and success criteria? Is this a regular part of our lessons? Have they had any experience with setting intentions for engagement?
- What skills do my students have that might support them to *participate* in planned learning activities? Get *invested* in what they are learning? Take on the *driving* pathway?

We also want to identify the things that are not yet happening or not working as well as they could, as this will help us to identify some next steps for helping students become more actively engaged in their learning. Here are some prompts to get you started:

- When reflecting on the earlier questions about engagement, did I identify some areas for improvement? What were they?
- How confident am I in my ability to effectively support students on each of the three engagement pathways? Where could I improve?
- How equipped are my students to manage their engagement and drive their learning forward? What skills do they need to develop?

SET YOUR INTENTION FOR ENGAGING IN LEARNING

As follows, you will find three suggested engagement pathways, but feel free to adapt them and make them your own. If you decide to write your own intention for how you will take your learning forward, see if you can then identify which engagement pathway that puts you on.

PARTICIPATING PATHWAY	INVESTING PATHWAY	DRIVING PATHWAY
I prefer to keep reading and learn a bit more before I look for ways to become more actively engaged in learning.	I have some questions that I want to investigate or some things that I want to discuss with my students/ colleagues. This will prepare me to take on the driving pathway.	I have identified some next steps for myself, and I have a clear idea of what I want to achieve. I am ready to make a plan and put it into action.

CHAPTER 5

Let's Tackle Disengagement!

"If they are not open and willing and have that mindset of 'I'm just going to give this a go,' then straightaway it's like they'll sit there and they won't do anything. Then the lesson loses its impact and power for learning. So, I guess it is a level of disengagement because it's not feeling comfortable and calm and open. And engagement is probably an openness to being able to learn new things even if it's challenging."

—Carol, sixth-grade teacher

Undoubtedly, student disengagement is one of the biggest challenges teachers face, and its negative impact on student learning, academic success, and overall well-being makes it one of the most pressing concerns for schools and teachers. While setting an intention to be disengaged is not something we want to encourage, we would be foolish to deny that from time to time we all end up on the disengaged side of the continuum. After all, we are not robots with uninterrupted supplies of motivation and energy that can be accessed at the flick of a switch. Sometimes engagement comes easy, and we feel quickly energized to dive into the challenge ahead of us. Other times, we have to work hard to find the energy and motivation to combat the forces of disengagement and get engaged. Equipping students with the skills to take their engagement from *participating* to *driving* is important, but we also need to prepare them to deal with the challenge of disengagement and share the responsibility for that as well. In this chapter, we will look at how we can help students to manage their disengagement in a way that supports their autonomy and agency and continues to value their input into the engagement partnership. In other words, how can we help them to want to choose to invest in learning? This includes changing the way we think and talk about disengagement in the classroom, developing a common language for disengagement, and collaborating with students to identify and develop strategies for addressing the underlying causes of disengagement. Extending the partnership approach to tackling disengagement and resisting the temptation to fall back into battle mode are the core elements we will focus on in this chapter.

PREVENTING AND RESPONDING TO DISENGAGEMENT

It is better to prevent disengagement wherever possible rather than having to respond to it once it has already happened. When students do choose to disengage, our goal is to help them energize and refocus their motivation to learn and their desire to engage in the learning activity. Whatever pathway of disengagement they are on, we want students to move onto a pathway of engaging. Realistically, this may involve a shift to *participating* before taking on the extra challenges involved with *investing* or *driving*, but looking ahead and setting our sights on *driving* may be a more effective way of charging up their motivation than setting a low ceiling of *participating*. Often it is the lack of desire to participate in the learning activity that is the root cause of *withdrawing*, *avoiding*, and *disrupting*. Hence, the aim is to help the students become more invested and interested in learning so that they want to choose to participate rather than disengage. The key to preventing and responding to disengagement is to nurture and build students' inner motivational resources and their capacity to take actions that will drive their learning forward—not to restrict their agency and attempt to force them into compliance.

CHANGING THE NARRATIVE AROUND DISENGAGEMENT

Before we rush in to tackle disengagement in our lessons, we need to take stock of where we are when talking about and responding to disengagement. We are looking to uncover the implicit and explicit messages about disengagement, the existing patterns of disengagement, and any existing barriers or contributors to disengagement in our classroom. Importantly, we want to know about the things that might contribute to a battle over disengagement rather than a partnership approach to disengagement.

REMOVING THE STIGMA OF DISENGAGEMENT—PROBLEM STUDENT OR STUDENT WITH A PROBLEM?

It does not take very long for students to learn that being disengaged translates to breaking the rules of the game of school. The rules are that students are expected to get involved in the activities that are planned, regardless of how they are feeling about it, and choosing to withhold that involvement is akin to willful disobedience. These "problem students" present a potential threat to the smooth running of the classroom or lesson and to the intentions the teacher has for teaching and learning. When there is a pattern of regular disengagement, the battle-weary teacher may opt to blame the "unmotivated" student for the unwillingness to engage and give up on trying to find a solution. This is made even easier if the student chooses to passively disengage as it removes the threat of disruption and often goes unnoticed by the teacher. From this perspective, disengagement is a problem that only applies to some students (those who choose to withhold their engagement) rather than something that all people experience at some time or another.

Let's take a minute to reflect on our own experiences of disengagement. Being able to connect with students over the human experience of feeling disengaged and unmotivated can help us destigmatize disengagement and see things from the learner's perspective.

A key feature of autonomy-supportive teaching is taking the perspective of the student. In this case, we are aiming to understand the student's experience of disengagement rather than seeing it only through the eyes of the teacher. As part of connecting with students about the experience of being disengaged, we might share our experiences of disengagement and the strategies we have found useful for dealing with disengagement. However, we must also include a genuine attempt to understand how our students are thinking and feeling if we are to work together to find a solution or strategy to support them.

TIME TO REFLECT

Asking everyone (teacher and students) to reflect on their experiences of disengagement and contribute to the discussion can help students realize that this is a challenge for all people, not just some. This could be a whole-group discussion, small-group discussions, or a jigsaw activity where students break into different groups to focus on different questions and then report back to their home group. Some prompts for reflection and discussion might be the following:

- What does it feel like when you are disengaged or unmotivated to learn?
- What thoughts do you have when you are disengaged or unmotivated to learn?
- What situations or activities do you find especially hard to get engaged in?
- What impact do your teachers have on your disengagement? How can they help? How can they make it worse?
- When you do not get involved, do you typically withdraw, actively avoid, or disrupt?
- What impact do your peers have on your disengagement? How can they help? How can they make it worse?
- What impact do you have on your disengagement? What things do you do that help you to engage? What things have you done that made it worse or prevented you from engaging?
- When you were learning at a distance (over the internet), did you disengage more or less than when in the classroom? If you disengaged more, what was different?

Don't forget to reflect on your experiences of disengagement as well so you can participate in the discussions.

KEY MESSAGE

All people experience challenges to their motivation and engagement, but some people are better at flying under the radar when disengaged or have better strategies for dealing with episodes of disengagement. The fact that certain students have never been labeled as disengaged at school does not mean they have never felt disengaged or adopted behaviors consistent with disengagement. This is especially true when we consider the passive form of *withdrawing*, where the aim is to go unnoticed and the behaviors are designed to not draw attention. All of us engage in selective listening, and this can be a powerful way of "turning off."

AVOIDING THE TEMPTATION TO CONTROL . . . AND BECOMING AWARE OF OUR CONTROLLING BEHAVIORS

This can be easier said than done! For many of us, the sight of an actively disengaged student sends us straight into "fix it quick" mode to avoid disruptions to the lesson or classroom. This can mean we fall into battle mode, using controlling strategies rather than strategies that support students to want to choose to engage in learning over disengaging from learning. Unfortunately, research tells us that when teachers are faced with disengagement, they tend to act in ways that make the situation worse rather than better, such as withdrawing support or attention and attempting to coerce the student into complying (Jang et al., 2016; Pelletier et al., 2002; Skinner & Belmont, 1993; Soenens et al., 2012). As Johnmarshall Reeve (2009) explained, when students demonstrate low motivation, low engagement, inattentiveness, or disruptive behavior, they can "push a teacher's buttons" in a way that causes the teacher to react in a more controlling way than normal (p. 166). Controlling practices can contribute to increases in both passive and active forms of student disengagement (Earl et al., 2017).

When faced with controlling teaching practices, students can develop a lack of confidence in their ability to successfully take on challenges in learning (Earl et al., 2017); experience increased levels of boredom, frustration, and disengagement (Skinner et al., 2008); have feelings of anger and anxiety (Assor et al., 2005); react with disobedience and disruptiveness (Earl et al., 2017); and tend to demonstrate fewer self-directed learning strategies that are correlated with achievement and academic performance (Soenens et al., 2012). When we try to coerce and control disengaged students, we not only inhibit their motivation and engagement in learning; we also inhibit their potential to make progress. Even more concerning, when teachers openly criticize, threaten, make sarcastic comments toward, or tease an individual student, it can result in an immediate decline in student engagement across the class, not just for the student at whom it is aimed (Strati et al., 2007).

Controlling behaviors include attempting to bribe students to comply, warning of negative consequences, withholding attention and support for disengaged students, and using language that is designed to control or shame the students into complying. Statements such as "You should have started by now," "I'm really disappointed—you need to do better than that," and "You have to focus and pay more attention" are all examples of compliance mandates. As we learned in Chapter 2, these things do nothing to energize the inner motivational resources of students, and instead frustrate the students' needs for autonomy, relatedness, and competence. Importantly, giving feedback, providing suggestions or recommendations, and clarifying instructions are not controlling behaviors in themselves. They become controlling when the teacher does not consider the student's perspective; attempts to pressure the student into thinking, feeling, or behaving in a certain way; or takes over in some way (e.g., taking materials away from a student, crossing things out on students' papers as they are working).

RELYING ON EVIDENCE, NOT INTUITION

It is common practice to gather evidence of their progress when we want to find out where students are in their learning and make decisions about what to do next. We can apply the same principles to engagement. Whether it is determining what level of engagement a student is operating at, who is disengaging from learning and why, or what impact our practices have on student engagement, relying on evidence rather than intuition is a more reliable path for improving student engagement.

Ideally, we aim to gather evidence from different perspectives or sources, using different strategies, and at different time points to cover any potential blind spots. For example, if teachers only rely on their observations during a lesson, they are likely to miss key aspects of engagement that are less easily observed such as emotions or inner motivation (Lee & Reeve,

2012; Skinner & Belmont, 1993). In this case, gathering additional evidence from the students themselves might complement the teacher observations to provide a fuller picture. Do you know the dominant feelings experienced by your students in class? Do you have a regular process in place for seeking feedback from students (e.g., using an app or exit ticket)? It is easy to fall into the trap of blaming students for disengagement, but we may be the source of their disengagement. Do you have a regular habit of following up with students to find out more about their disengagement? Do you ask for feedback on things that you might be doing to contribute to their disengagement? Seeking regular input from students on their experience of learning can help to uncover important information that can be used to improve the quality of teaching and the level of engagement in learning.

Similarly, teachers might not be aware of the controlling language they use when interacting with some students, but this could be picked up by a trusted colleague during a lesson observation. Being able to see things in the classroom with fresh eyes can help us to uncover things about engagement that were previously hidden to us, and reflecting on this new knowledge can help us to improve.

There are different ways we can gather and use evidence about engagement, and you may need to experiment with different strategies to explore the benefits and limitations of each. Aim to have multiple strategies for collecting evidence of student engagement, as one strategy will not provide you with all of the information that you need.

Some strategies for gathering evidence related to engagement are described as follows:

The buddy system—Partner with a colleague and take turns observing each other's lessons (these can be in-person observations or observations of lesson videos). Meet ahead of time to decide on the focus for the observation. Ideally, the person being observed will identify an area of focus for improvement. For example, the teacher might ask the observer to focus on potential *withdrawing* behaviors during lessons to improve the awareness of disengaged students who might be less visible. Ask your buddy to identify some *withdrawing* students, and note when they began to turn off, what they did, and whether they participated in any parts of the lesson to find out what turned them off and on. Or, the observer might be asked to focus on the teacher's responses to disengagement during the lesson as a way of uncovering any controlling behaviors that might be contributing to the problem. Of course, this requires trust and respect between you and your buddy if it is going to work. Having three columns for observation notes is a good idea. One column is reserved for the observation, one column for the interpretation, and one column for any questions that arise while observing. Meeting afterward to discuss is key, as this is where the reflecting and learning happens. Be on the lookout for things that you have not noticed yourself, and interpretations that might differ from your own, as these can be powerful learning moments. The aim is for collaborative reflection and discussion, with both parties actively engaged in the process.

Video-supported reflection—An alternative is to video your lessons and use this recording to support your reflection. You can use the same process that was described earlier for taking observation notes, providing you with a record of your practice and thinking. When interpreting things that you see and hear, ask yourself if there are other possible interpretations. How might someone else interpret the same student or situation? Being able to refer back to these pieces of evidence can help you to evaluate the impact your improvement efforts are having on student engagement and see the changes to your practice and thinking over time. Sharing your observations, reflections, and goals for improvement with colleagues and your students can help you take the process one step further, enabling you to *drive* your progress forward with the help of feedback and support from others.

Feedback from students—Students are our partners in engagement and a valuable source of information when we are gathering evidence. There are many strategies we can use to get input from students, and the key is to think about what you want to know and how best to find that out. For example:

- Asking students to rate their level of engagement at different points in a lesson
- Asking students to give feedback on the motivating and demotivating aspects of a learning activity (e.g., what made them want to engage, what made it hard for them to engage)
- Asking students for feedback on your practice (e.g., things you do that help them get more engaged, things you do that make them feel like disengaging)
- Asking students for suggestions on how the activity could be improved to make it more engaging

Using exit tickets or exit slips is another great way of gathering input from students. Exit slips fall into three categories (Fisher & Frey, 2004):

- Prompts that document learning

  Example: Write one thing you learned today.

  Example: Discuss how today's lesson could be used in the real world.

- Prompts that emphasize the process of learning

  Example: I didn't understand . . .

  Example: Write one question you have about today's lesson.

- Prompts to evaluate the effectiveness of instruction

  Example: Did you enjoy working in small groups today?

KEY MESSAGE

Not many teachers would readily identify themselves as controlling, but we know that this is a common practice, especially in response to disengagement in the classroom. We are not always aware of our patterns of responding to disengagement or interacting with students who appear regularly disengaged in classroom activities. Similarly, we may be unaware of student patterns of disengagement, especially students who appear to be *participating* in activities but are actually *withdrawing* from learning. Rather than assume you know what is going on, collect some evidence to help you better understand what is happening in your class.

PASSIVE DOES NOT MEAN LESS SERIOUS

While there are similarities to both sides of the engagement continuum, namely that both disengagement and engagement have passive and active forms, there are important differences. First, more active engagement is likely to facilitate greater gains in learning, but the same does not hold true for disengagement. That is, students do not learn less if they are *avoiding* than if they are *withdrawing*. The students' choice not to invest in learning is what puts their learning at risk, not the choice of what they will do instead. Spending ten minutes searching through a backpack to avoid working is no more detrimental to learning than spending ten minutes staring out of the window and daydreaming. The forms of disengaging may look different, but the impact on learning is the same: Compliant but passively disengaged students do just as poorly on average as students who are more actively disengaged (Angus et al., 2009). Worryingly, the pervasiveness of passive disengagement in classrooms makes it a serious concern, with many teachers reporting it to be a daily challenge (Sullivan et al., 2014). While *disrupting* may be less common, its effect on learning and engagement can spread. When students choose to engage in behaviors that disrupt and distract others, the impact on learning increases as it extends beyond the individual who is disengaged and puts the learning of others at risk as well.

The second key difference between engagement and disengagement has to do with motivation to learn. When students demonstrate increasing levels of engagement, this behavior is fueled by rising levels of motivation to learn. Students on the *driving* pathway are investing more inner motivational resources into learning than students on the *participating* pathway. But, we cannot say that students who are *disrupting* are more unmotivated to learn than those who are *withdrawing*, and it is not the case that the more unmotivated to learn they are, the more actively disengaged they will be. Many students will never get to the level of trying to disrupt the learning environment, no matter how unmotivated to learn they feel. There are other factors at play when students decide to do something instead of engaging in learning. Working with students to explore their individual patterns of disengagement can help both of you become better prepared to notice the signs of disengagement and develop strategies for preventing or responding to disengagement in the future.

KEY MESSAGE

Withdrawing is a serious concern due to its detrimental effect on student learning and the pervasive yet often hidden nature of this form of disengagement. It is easy to miss the signs of *withdrawing* or mistake *withdrawing* for *participating*. Teachers need to actively look for the signs of passive disengagement, seek input and insights from students about *withdrawing*, and work together to shine a spotlight on this "under the radar" form of disengagement.

ACKNOWLEDGING AND
ACCEPTING NEGATIVE FEELINGS

Disengagement frequently involves negative feelings about learning or complaints about the learning activity. For example, students might complain that it is too boring, say it is too much work, or question why they are being asked to do it. When students complain, teachers often attempt to control them by shutting them down, dismissing them, or trying to force them to feel or think differently. Suppressing student criticism thwarts rather than enhances student motivation and engagement in learning (Assor, 2012). Instead, we can take the autonomy-supportive path by acknowledging the negative feeling, accepting this feeling as valid, and asking for suggestions to address the cause of the negative feeling (Reeve, 2016). Here is an example of how a teacher might respond to negative feelings in either a controlling or an autonomy-supportive way:

CONTROLLING RESPONSE	AUTONOMY-SUPPORTIVE RESPONSE
"Come on, everyone, get to work and stop wasting time. Harry, stop complaining. You know what to do, so get going. Sometimes we have to do boring things—that's life."	"Okay, it looks like a lot of people are struggling with this activity and finding it not so engaging. And yes, Harry, I can see your point. We have done this same thing many times before. Does anyone have a suggestion for how we might do it a bit differently this time?"

As the teacher, you might need to take the first step in suggesting a change to the activity or instructions. This shows you are respecting the engagement partnership and are willing to take on feedback and find ways to improve engagement in the activity. If students are feeling stressed, angry, frustrated, or confused, they might not be ready or able to share their ideas and may benefit from hearing your suggestion first as a starting point in the dialogue (Reeve, 2016).

KEY MESSAGE

Negative emotions like anger, frustration, anxiety, and stress are often present when students become disengaged from learning. It can be challenging for the teacher to respond to student complaints and negative

(Continued)

(Continued)

responses to a task or instruction, and the inclination may be to control and suppress them as quickly as possible to minimize the threat of disrupting the lesson. As with other controlling behaviors, this is likely to make things worse rather than better. The teacher may be successful in forcing students into compliance in the short term, but this approach threatens our relationship with students and the engagement partnership we are trying to build.

SNAPSHOT OF PRACTICE

Sometimes students resist taking an active role in their engagement and want to remain in the passive passenger mode, even if this is contributing to their disengagement from learning and school. Lauren, a fifth-grade teacher, describes one such experience with a student in her class:

I have one student who was really disengaged. For the first two terms, he went home every day and said, "School is boring. I hate school. I don't see the point. Why do I have to go?" And I tried so many things with him just to find some sort of trigger for him to just be interested, to just try and engage him a little bit more and get him to want to drive his own learning. He would resist and get frustrated and say, "Just tell me what to do, and I'll do it. Whatever." And I thought, no, I don't want to do that. So I started saying, "What are you going to do? How are you going to do it? This is the expectation. How are you going to exceed it?"

He started taking more responsibility for his learning and making choices about things he was interested in learning about, rather than waiting to be told what to do. He even started helping other students. It was amazing. What he needed from me was to not accept him taking a passive role and putting in minimal effort. He started realizing that more was expected of him and that he was capable of more. Last term, for the first time, he said, "I'm proud of what I've accomplished." That was huge. He's started doing other things like reading at home and having conversations about what he's learning. His mother told me he still goes home sometimes saying things are boring, so I asked him about it. He shrugged his shoulders and said, "I get home and I'm tired and I don't want to talk so I just say it." We're still working on it, but he has come a long way.

CHECKING IN ON DISENGAGEMENT

During the process of checking in, we are looking for evidence of how the student is engaging in learning, and also any evidence that the student is disengaging from learning. Checking in on disengagement involves two objectives, pinpointing the behaviors that indicate the student is disengaging and finding out what is keeping the student from engaging. Whether we are checking in as a whole class or checking in with an individual student, the aim is to engage in a discussion with both teacher and student sharing ideas, observations, and thinking. The following prompts give some indication of what we want to touch on in our discussions around disengagement:

- If you have observed some signs that the student might be disengaged, share them in a noncontrolling way ("I noticed you seem to be having a hard time getting engaged with this task. Shall we do a check-in?").

- Ask them to evaluate their engagement ("Where would you say your engagement is right now? What pathway do you think you are on? What makes you think that?").

- Ask them what you can do to help ("How can I help you to get engaged?").

- Ask them what they can do to help themselves ("What is something you could do to help yourself get engaged?").

CHECKING IN ON WITHDRAWING

"I am choosing not to engage in the learning activity, but I will try to appear compliant so the teacher won't notice me."

When students are *withdrawing* from learning, they are attempting to fly under the radar and disengage from the learning activity without being noticed by the teacher. They may be attempting to avoid confrontation with the teacher over their lack of engagement or having to deal with any attempt by the teacher to force them to engage. This can involve withdrawing attention (e.g., thinking about other things), withdrawing effort (e.g., doing just enough to go unnoticed by the teacher), or withdrawing motivation (e.g., not caring about making progress). Many of us are quite familiar with this form of disengaging and can probably think of many times we have found ourselves physically present but mentally and emotionally elsewhere. For example, when I'm sitting in meetings that seem to have no purpose or relevance to me, I struggle to get involved or pay attention and find myself making lists or thinking about other things.

Passive students do not pose an immediate threat to the learning environment, and generally do not receive the same amount of attention from the teacher or their peers as students who are actively engaged (Paulsen et al., 2006). If we want to find out if students are *withdrawing*, we have to look for the signs, as it is not as obvious as *avoiding* or *disrupting*. The nature of this form of disengaging means that the observable signs are often subtle and other signs will be felt internally by the student but may not be observable by others. For this reason, we must collaborate with students to look for the signs of *withdrawing*.

Some of the signs of *withdrawing* that students and teachers might look out for are the following:

> *I am thinking about other things.*
>
> *I am staring out the window or into space.*
>
> *I am drawing or doodling to pass the time.*
>
> *I am watching the clock and waiting for the lesson to be over.*
>
> *I pretend to work when the teacher comes near me.*
>
> *I am pretending to listen and pay attention.*
>
> *I am choosing to sit away from the group or at the back.*
>
> *I am choosing not to get involved in group discussions or activities.*
>
> *I put minimal effort into my work.*
>
> *I don't care about learning this.*
>
> *I am bored.*

You can work with your students to adapt these statements or add more to create a description of the *withdrawing* pathway that is meaningful and relevant to your class.

TAKING IT INTO THE CLASSROOM

Withdrawing can be very subtle and easily goes unnoticed in a busy classroom. As teachers, we have to work hard to uncover the many ways that students *withdraw* from learning. We can start by asking them to reflect on times when they found themselves *withdrawing* and describe the things they tend to do when they are on this pathway. Given how common this form of disengaging is, it is likely that most students will have some experience with it. Facilitating open discussions about *withdrawing* can help students to become more aware of it and may also help us to become more aware of the cues that signal passive disengagement from learning in our classroom.

One activity you might try with your students is a *Looks like/Feels like/ Sounds like* thinking routine and record the students' responses on a Y-chart like the one pictured. The completed chart can be used to support discussions about *withdrawing* and during the checking-in process.

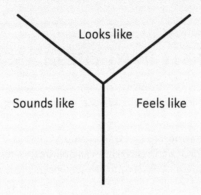

CHECKING IN ON AVOIDING

"I am choosing not to engage in the learning activity, and I will actively try to avoid it for as long as possible."

At the *avoiding* level of disengaging, students are less concerned with going unnoticed and are instead focused on finding ways of actively avoiding the task or activity that has been planned. This form of disengaging is often associated with "off-task" behavior. You might have already noticed that some of your students have regular patterns of avoiding—for example, the student who always needs to go and get something from their bag as soon as it is time to start a task or the student who has a habit of engaging in off-task talking during group activities. There are many common strategies that students use to avoid, including moving around the room unnecessarily, asking to leave the room, taking a long time to get their materials ready, and talking with their friends. Some strategies are more unique to the individual student. When I taught fourth grade, I had a student who was such an avid reader that I often found him with his head in his desk reading a book during math lessons.

Some of the behaviors you might find on the *avoiding* pathway include the following:

I am looking for ways to procrastinate.

I am looking for reasons to leave the room or move around the room.

I choose not to come prepared with the things I need to get to work.

I am choosing to do other things rather than the work.

I am playing around with others or with materials.

I am talking with others about things that don't relate to what we are learning.

TAKING IT INTO THE CLASSROOM

Ask students to describe the strategies they use to avoid engaging in an activity or task and add these to the *avoiding* pathway to make it more useful during checking in. Some students may never move beyond *withdrawing* in the classroom and therefore have less personal examples of *avoiding* to draw upon. However, this form of disengaging is less subtle and students should be able to easily describe things that students sometimes do or might do when they are trying to avoid working. You might also extend the discussion to look at the different strategies they use to avoid engaging in activities outside of school (e.g., avoiding homework).

CHECKING IN ON DISRUPTING

"I am choosing not to engage in the learning activity and choosing to disrupt others from engaging in it as well."

Students at the *disrupting* level are demonstrating the most active form of disengagement. They are actively behaving in ways that disrupt the learning environment and distract or prevent other students from learning. They are not concerned with drawing attention to themselves and might be trying to get attention through their behavior. This has the potential to negatively impact learning across the class and not just for the student who is *disrupting*. The visibility of these behaviors and the potential threat they present to teaching and learning mean teachers are often quick to react to this form of disengagement.

Some of the behaviors you might find on the *disrupting* pathway are these:

I am looking for ways to disrupt the teacher from teaching.

I am looking for ways to disrupt other students who are working.

I am refusing to participate or work.

I am arguing with the teacher or with other people in the class.

I am trying to distract others from their work.

I am trying to start a fight with other students.

TAKING IT INTO THE CLASSROOM

Given this is the most extreme form of disengagement, many students will not be able to describe times when they tried to *disrupt* the lesson or learning. They may be able to describe examples they have witnessed (focusing on the behavior, not the person), and explain what impact it had on them. The goal here is to describe the behaviors associated with the *disrupting pathway* (as we have done with each of the other forms of engagement) and the impact it has on others while not turning it into an attack on individuals who may have a history of *disrupting*.

One activity you might try is to describe a short vignette of a student *disrupting*. You can tailor this to suit your context and the students you teach so that it will be meaningful for them. Facilitate a discussion to clarify what happened in the story, and what behaviors were demonstrated that indicate the student is on the *disrupting pathway*. To help everyone see how this form of disengagement affects other people, too, work with the students to come up with a list of different perspectives or viewpoints to think about the story from. For example, you could consider the perspectives of the student who is *disrupting*, the teacher, other students in the class, and the class next door. Select a viewpoint to explore (this could be done as a whole class or in groups) and respond to the thinking prompts *I am thinking* . . . and *I am feeling* . . . Record student responses and facilitate a discussion to identify the common threads and the differences in the different viewpoints.

The activities described earlier are aimed at shining a spotlight on the different ways that students can disengage from learning and at preparing students to share the responsibility for solving the challenge of disengagement. That is not to suggest that the activities cannot be adapted and extended to explore the different engagement pathways as well. For example, using a vignette describing a student who is *driving* and then looking at it from different perspectives could be an effective way of exploring the positive influence this form of engagement can have on different members of the classroom community. Similarly, using the *Looks like/Feels like/Sounds like* activity to look at both *withdrawing* and *participating* might be a good way of considering the similarities and differences between these two passive forms.

GETTING TO THE HEART OF THE PROBLEM

While disengagement may come in different forms, there are some common reasons why students choose to disengage in the first place. We have already looked at controlling teacher practices that contribute to disengagement. These practices frustrate rather than support students' inner motivational resources and contribute to both passive and active forms of disengagement. Let's look at some of the other barriers to engagement commonly experienced by students.

TOO HARD

When a learning activity is pitched at a level that is beyond what students can successfully accomplish, or it is not clear to students what they have to do or how to do it, it can threaten their motivation to want to engage with it. Why bother to invest in a task where the likelihood of success or finishing is so remote that it is easier to not engage at all?

This roadblock can also occur when students have a low level of confidence in their ability to achieve success, feel pressured to get the right answer and deliver it quickly, and are averse to taking on challenges. When a task is too hard (or perceived as being too hard), students' need for competence will likely be frustrated, as will their need to feel like success is within their control (autonomy), and it damages their trust in the teacher as a partner in learning (relatedness). When the instructions and expectations for a task have not been clearly explained, this can also frustrate students' need to feel like we are there for them and are willing to do our part to support them in taking on the challenge of learning. While we want enough challenge within an activity to require some effort and hard thinking, if it is too hard, a student might choose to disengage instead of risking failure and frustration.

Here are suggestions for tackling the "too hard" barrier:

- Communicate clear intentions for learning, provide clear instructions, describe the pathway to success, and support students to set an intention for engaging.

- Know your students, know where they are in their learning, know their patterns and characteristics as learners (including patterns of disengaging and engaging), and anticipate the potential barriers for individual students that relate to the perceived challenge of an activity.

- Differentiate learning activities to accommodate the diversity within your class, and provide options for different engagement pathways and different pathways of success so that all students are supported to feel that success is possible and within their control.

- Demonstrate patience and give students the time they need to learn at their own pace.

- Check in with students and monitor the level of challenge, working with them to find the best path for engagement and learning.

- Support students to develop a positive view of challenge and struggle, resilience to mistakes and failures, and strategies for seeking help when the challenge becomes too hard, avoiding the temptation to rescue students from thinking hard.

TOO EASY

Just as students can be turned off by work that is too hard, so too can they be turned off by work that is too easy. Graham Nuthall (2007) explored the insides of classrooms for many years and found that students already know 40 to 50 percent of what teachers cover during lessons. For high-ability students, the problem can be considerably worse when they are continuously tasked with doing things that they have already mastered. As one student reflected, "I could sleep through class and still do well because it was geared so below me" (Fredricks et al., 2010, p. 25). However, this is not just a problem for high-ability students. Students of all abilities can experience the demotivating effects of low teacher expectations and work that is easily completed with minimal effort. Some students welcome challenges and want to be part of discovering new ideas, as this experience energizes their motivation to learn and drives them toward wanting to engage. Repetitive, easy work is a great incentive for these students to become disengaged. When work is too easy, students can disengage and still get it done, or may simply choose to opt out altogether.

It is not just about selecting appropriately challenging tasks, but also about how those tasks are implemented in the classroom. A research program documenting typical teaching practices in different countries found that teachers in the United States (and Australia to a lesser degree) decreased the level of challenge during implementation by turning a math problem that required students to engage in higher-order thinking into one that only asked them to apply basic computational skills and procedures (Stigler & Hiebert, 2004).

Here are strategies for tackling the "too easy" barrier:

- Use preassessment strategies to help you target your instruction and select appropriate learning activities. A good preassessment task will identify what students know and can do (providing a foundation on which to build), as well as what they don't understand or can't do yet (illuminating areas for learning and improvement). If a student has already learned something, there is little sense in teaching it again. It is time for you and the student to move on.

- When choosing learning activities, think about how you can increase the level of challenge during the lesson as needed. What could you do to make it more challenging? How could you prompt deeper thinking and more active engagement?

- Ask students for their ideas on how to transform a "too easy" activity into one that challenges their thinking and makes them want to get engaged.

- Be aware of things you might be doing that turn a challenging activity into a "too easy" activity. Are you taking away the opportunity for students to engage in hard thinking? Are you preventing students from engaging in productive struggle as they try to work through a problem? Are you changing the goalpost from thinking hard to following instructions?

- Ask students for feedback on their preferences for challenging work and their experiences of being challenged in your class. How often do they feel challenged to think hard during lessons? How would they rate the level of challenge in lessons—too hard, too easy, or just right?

- Monitor the level of challenge during learning by seeking input from the students. Make a habit of finding out who wants to be more challenged or who is ready to tackle a bigger challenge.

Finding the right level of challenge for students will depend on many things, not just their current level of skill and knowledge. It is also influenced by things like their confidence as a learner, their capacity to take on challenges and persist through periods of struggle, their strategies for seeking help, and their motivation to want to engage in the activity in the first place (e.g., interest, curiosity, personal value or relevance). Digging into the details of what "too hard" or "too easy" means for each student and getting to know all your students, including their preferences and patterns of responding to challenges, is key to finding a solution.

TOO BORING

At the risk of pointing out the obvious, it is hard to get motivated and excited about an inherently boring task. Boredom among adolescents has been on the rise over the past decade, especially for girls (Weybright et al., 2020), and, sadly, many activities at school can be repetitive or dull and do nothing to energize student motivation to learn. I remember clearly the battles I had with my son over the weekly task of writing out his spelling words four times—it was an unwelcome chore for both of us. As a teacher, it was clear that working through a set of addition problems from the board was never going to be met with the same amount of enthusiasm as a real-world investigation that required students to use addition. Highlighting the persuasive techniques in a written text was never going to be as interesting as using those techniques to convince the principal that a trip to the theme park would be a great way to learn about physics.

Tackling boredom is not about teachers entertaining students or making everything fun for them—remember students are our partners in engagement. Instead, we want to try and see the activity from their perspective and integrate elements designed to energize their motivation to choose engagement over disengagement.

Does the activity connect with student interests or things they find important and valuable? Does it have relevance to their lives outside the classroom?

Does the activity put a ceiling on engagement, limiting it to participating?

Does the activity facilitate hard thinking, curiosity, or creativity?

Does the activity empower students to be actively involved in decisions about what they will learn and how they will learn it?

Are there opportunities for students to interact and support each other during learning?

Asking ourselves these questions while planning can help us to avoid the curse of "too boring." Triggering their interest in learning puts students on a pathway to actively engaging in that activity and sets in motion a pattern of active engagement beyond that activity (Pattal et al., 2016), making it a worthwhile strategy for tackling disengagement.

Boring can be code for different things. Lessons that force students into a passive state of listening, watching, responding, and following instructions are very familiar and routine to students and do little to inspire curiosity, interest, or a desire to choose to engage in learning. The content itself might be perceived as boring, and even more so when it is presented in a boring way. If the activity is too far beyond the students, this can lead to boredom because they have nothing to grab onto that might interest them or get them thinking. As with the "too hard" barrier, we need to dig a little deeper into what "too boring" means to understand what is getting in the way of engagement. Ideally, we want to avoid this barrier altogether if we can. Planning to prevent boredom is easier than having to respond to boredom once it has taken hold, especially if that boredom is felt across the classroom and extends beyond one activity.

Tips for tackling the "too boring" barrier include the following:

- Minimize activities that limit students to passive compliance and thus put a ceiling of *participation* on student engagement.

- Build in strategies that aim to take thinking to a deeper level and experiment with using these strategies at different points in the lesson or learning process. For example, try using a curiosity-provoking question at the start of a lesson and see what impact that has on student engagement. What happens if you use that strategy at the end of a lesson as a lead-in to the next day? Can students come up with their own "I wonder" questions to take the group's thinking deeper?

- Understand each student's tolerance for challenge, and teach those with low tolerance coping strategies to take on a greater level of challenge.

- Look for ways of connecting what the students are learning to their lives in and outside of school in meaningful ways. For example, try using a text as a stimulus to explore a concept such as friendship, conflict, or justice. Or, get the students involved in a citizen science project to connect with a topic you are learning in science or social studies.

- Rather than sticking to the same structure in each lesson—such as teaching a skill or concept and then giving an activity where the students apply it—try mixing things up a bit by introducing an open-ended exploration or provocation to get students actively thinking from the start rather than heading down the familiar path of disengaging while they wait for their turn to do something. Introducing elements of uncertainty into lessons can increase curiosity, and support both deeper learning and transfer of learning to a new context (Lamnina & Chase, 2019).

- Build in opportunities for students to work together and learn from each other as a way of improving motivation and learning. This is a key characteristic of the *investing* and *driving* levels of engagement, and we will look at it in more detail in the next chapter.

WHY BOTHER?

Most of us have had the experience of sitting in a meeting, watching a presentation, or being in a workshop and thinking, "Who cares? What is the point of this? Why would I want to do this? What does this have to do with me?" If you can relate to this, then you will appreciate the "why bother" challenge. When students cannot see the point of investing their effort and motivation into a learning activity, see no value or interest in it, or feel it has no relevance to their goals or life, this presents a significant barrier to engagement—particularly if the expectation is to move beyond *participating*. Importantly, this does not mean you have to connect *every* activity to students' lives or their aspirations for the future. It means showing the students how the task or skill relates to other tasks or skills, relates to the success criteria of the lesson, and is a skill necessary in a progression. Showing them the worthwhileness and purpose of the activity is what matters.

Autonomy-supportive teachers make an effort to elicit and integrate student interests, preferences, and needs into the flow of learning—enabling the students to avoid the "why bother" barrier or respond to it when it arises. They also provide explanations that communicate the reasoning and usefulness behind what they are asking the students to do. They answer the question of "why bother" as a part of the process of instruction. This is especially important if the activity is not inherently interesting or connected to things that are meaningful and important to the students.

> *"Explanatory rationales are not contrived excuses for learning but are, instead, scaffolds to help students mentally transform the uninteresting or unvalued activities they face in the classroom into something of greater personal value."*
>
> —Johnmarshall Reeve (2009, pp. 169–170)

Here are ideas for tackling the "why bother" barrier:

- Take the students' perspective to identify potential "why bother" feelings; look for ways to connect with their interests, things they value, and goals they have for themselves; and seek their input and feedback on what you are planning.

- When asking students to do something that is not inherently interesting, valuable, or meaningful to them, provide a rationale to explain why it will be useful or necessary as part of the instruction. This might include making a connection between the current task and something more interesting and motivating that will follow (e.g., "We are going to do this now to help us get ready for . . .").

- Acknowledge and accept negative feelings or responses, then invite student input into finding a solution that works for both of you. Providing critical feedback and identifying a problem is the easy part, but as engagement partners, students also need to be part of the solution.

- Be flexible and open to making adjustments in response to student input. For example, if students are frustrated by having to work through a worksheet of practice problems and want to move straight into a more challenging task, you might suggest they do one of the practice problems to check for themselves that they are ready and then let them move on. Agree to check in with them once they have gotten started to see how it is going.

TOO DISTRACTED

At times, students may experience distractions that prevent them from engaging in a learning activity. This might be an external distraction, such as a disruption in the classroom, interference from another student, or something in the environment that interferes with their ability to concentrate and think (e.g., noise, heat, movement). It might also take the form of an internal distraction, such as anxiety, anger, sadness, or feeling unwell. This barrier is a little different from the others. Students may have less control over the things that are distracting them from learning and may have to rely on others to help them overcome the distraction. It may be a one-off distraction (e.g., they had a fight with a friend just before the lesson), or it may be a more persistent and ongoing distraction (e.g., anxiety relating to a particular subject or type of activity).

Suggestions for tackling the "too distracted" barrier include the following:

- Communicate clear expectations for student behavior, hold students accountable for their behavior choices, monitor for the early signs that students might be distracting others, and intervene early and give the students a chance to reflect on their behavior and make a different choice.

- Get to know individual students and any ongoing challenges that frequently distract them from learning, get to know the signs that they are distracted, and work with them to develop strategies that help them to overcome the distraction and get engaged in learning.

- Be on the lookout for indicators of distraction, which might include signs that students are upset, angry, frustrated, or focused on something that is happening around them, or behaviors related to *withdrawing*.

- When the problem is beyond the scope of what you can deal with on your own (e.g., highly aggressive and disruptive behavior, mental health issues), reach out for help to support the student and yourself.

Unfortunately, students may be battling multiple barriers at one time, making it even more difficult to get engaged. For example, students might see the task as both boring and too hard, making it even more likely that they will choose to disengage from it. Or, an activity might be seen as both boring and of no value whatsoever to a student, making it hard for that student to want to invest any effort into it. We need to take into account the combination of reasons why students have chosen to disengage if we are going to be able to plan a pathway forward with them. *I want to do it, but I'm not sure how to go about it or if I can succeed* is very different from *I don't care about this at all, and I don't think I can do it anyway.* While both involve a "too hard" barrier, addressing this barrier alone may be insufficient for the student who also sees no point in the activity and has no interest in learning from it.

TAKING IT INTO THE CLASSROOM

This is not an exhaustive list of all the reasons why students disengage; it is meant to highlight some of the common reasons. Work with your students to come up with your own list of barriers. You can use a T-chart such as the following to identify both the roadblocks to engaging and the things that promote disengagement:

THINGS THAT MAKE IT HARD FOR ME TO GET ENGAGED	THINGS THAT MAKE ME WANT TO DISENGAGE

Get the students to help you group responses that are similar, and turn this into your list of barriers to engagement. You can compare that to the barriers we have considered in this chapter to look for similarities and differences.

Once you have created a list, ask each student to identify the most common challenges that make it hard for them to get engaged in learning activities. Depending on the list and the age of the students, you might ask for their number-one challenge or their top three challenges. This can provide valuable information about the engagement patterns and needs of individual students in your classroom, as well as useful feedback on your engagement practices.

EXTENDING THE ENGAGEMENT PARTNERSHIP

Tackling student disengagement is perhaps one of the biggest challenges facing teachers, particularly if we are stuck in battle mode and cannot see a way out. It might seem too good to be true that students who are frequently disengaged will be willing and capable of sharing the responsibility for their disengagement and for finding solutions that will make them want to engage and learn. You might also be skeptical about the practicality of autonomy-supportive teaching, believing it is good in theory but simply too hard to implement in practice. If this is you, take heart. Many teachers have been in the same position, and after improving their understanding of and skills in autonomy-supportive teaching, they now believe it is easy once you know how to do it (Reeve & Cheon, 2016).

It can pay to extend the engagement partnership beyond teacher and students, especially when it comes to tackling disengagement. We've already looked at some of the ways you can partner with colleagues to support improvements relating to disengagement. You might find it is also useful to invite other members of the school community (e.g., school counselors, leadership) and parents into the partnership to provide additional support for you and your students. In the same way that we expect students to seek help when they need it, you also need to reach out to others when you feel you need more support to deal with the challenges of disengagement.

CHAPTER 6

Peers as Partners in Engagement

"Peers can be fantastic. You can have that group where they are all motivated and excited about working together, and you can see they really thrive in that situation. But, sometimes, peers can cause roadblocks in learning. I think it's more of the social stuff that can cause that. That's where I can immediately see whether or not they have good cooperative skills or good teamwork skills. You can see leaders straight away, or you can see followers, or you can see the person who always just kind of hides. A lot of them can get quite disgruntled and upset when placed into different groups that aren't necessarily with their friends."

—Joe, middle school teacher

When I asked teachers about the role peers play in student engagement, the responses were mixed. Many teachers acknowledged the potential for greater engagement when students work together, but they also spoke in detail about the roadblocks, challenges, and barriers to engagement and learning during group activities—particularly for students who are working with friends. One thing teachers did agree on was that peers can be a powerful influence on student engagement during learning experiences, sometimes influencing greater levels of engagement and other times contributing to disengagement. In previous chapters, we looked at how students interact with their peers at different levels of engagement. At the *participating* level, students may interact but only if instructed to do so by the teacher. At the *investing* level, students begin to share their ideas and insights because they find learning interesting and want to talk about it with someone. At the *driving* level, we begin to see the real value of peer interactions because they are focused on thinking deeper, understanding more, and making improvements—in other words, learning. When students are engaged at this level, they work as partners and take actions that help them progress toward their learning goals. Unfortunately, when students are disengaged, this can contribute to the disengagement of other students. Students who are *disrupting* can distract others and make it hard for them to engage, as can students who are *avoiding* work by playing around or talking about things unrelated to the learning focus. When students choose to *withdraw* during a group or pair activity, it might cause others in the group to feel frustrated or angry at having to do all of the work rather than energized and wanting to learn.

TIME TO REFLECT

Take a moment to reflect on your own experiences in the classroom.

Can you recall times when students had a positive impact on the engagement of their peers? What was the impact?

Have you had experiences where students had a negative impact on the engagement of their peers? What was the impact?

In this chapter, we will start by looking at the types of social interaction characteristic of the different forms of engagement and look more closely at what it means to be *driving together* during group learning experiences. After that, we will look at what the research says about the effect of peers on motivation and engagement. Finally, we will explore the possibilities of extending our engagement partnership beyond teacher and student to include partnering with peers for engagement. Expanding the network of engagement partners means students can have greater access to support when they need it, and this can contribute to a greater feeling of connection and cohesiveness as we begin to share the responsibility for engagement across the whole group.

ENGAGING WITH PEERS DURING LEARNING

In Chapter 1, we were introduced to the engagement continuum and the different forms that engagement and disengagement can take in a classroom. For each form of engagement, we can describe how students engage with the learning activity and how they engage with their peers during the learning activity. In Chapters 4 and 5, we looked at the different ways that students engage with or disengage from the planned learning activity. Now we will focus on how students engage with their peers during learning.

PARTICIPATING WITH PEERS

We are doing things together.

At the *participating* level, students only interact with other students as directed by the teacher. For example, they complete work with a partner or in a group because they were instructed to do so. At this level, the students are not acting with agency and autonomy to direct their own progress and engagement in learning. Instead, they are relying on the teacher (or a peer) to lead. Students who are *participating together* are focused on *doing together* rather than *thinking together* or *learning together*, which may limit the potential for peers to influence motivation and engagement unless someone chooses to take the engagement to a higher level (e.g., *investing*) or selects a path of disengaging.

Participating in a social learning environment involves following the classroom rules and norms, contributing to discussions when called on, cooperating with others to complete tasks when asked to, and following the processes and procedures that have been established.

INVESTING WITH PEERS

We are thinking about things together.

At the *investing* level, social interaction with peers becomes an important part of how students engage in the learning activity. This involves sharing ideas, insights, knowledge, and questions. Importantly, it is about wanting to share these things, not just doing it because the teacher says so. We *want* to share our excitement when a discovery is made. We *want* to share our questions and the things that puzzle us or make us wonder. We *want* to share our thinking, and we can see the value in thinking together as a way of moving forward. Along with that, it can be exciting and enjoyable when someone wants to share those things with us—which can help us get more interested, more motivated, and more engaged. Teachers may initially facilitate and support this behavior as part of the design of the activity (e.g., using a *Think-Pair-Share* strategy to come up with questions for the group to investigate) or by noticing and encouraging this type of behavior when they see it (e.g., "Fantastic to see this group sharing their ideas about what to do next! They are definitely on an *investing* pathway"). But ultimately, to get to *investing*, the students will be motivated to do these things because they see the value in it for themselves. They are doing it because they want to, not because they have to, as one teacher described:

"The way that they relate to other students says a lot about their engagement, I think. The questioning—I think questioning's a big thing—if I hear kids questioning each other and, you know, debating issues and sharing opinions and that sort of thing, I find that's a higher level of engagement because it's not just a passive listening to somebody and then I share what I think because 'that's what the teacher said we have to do.' It's actually adding to what others have said and sometimes challenging them. 'Yeah, I see what you are saying, but have you thought about this?'"

If you are not sure what the motivation is behind these social interactions during learning, ask the students to explain why they chose to share ideas or come up with questions together. Is it because that was the instruction from you, or is it because they see it as an action that will help them engage and make progress?

Investing in a social learning environment involves choosing to interact with others as a way of energizing motivation and making progress in learning. This includes exchanging ideas and opinions, sharing things that interest us or make us wonder, listening to different perspectives and ways of thinking as a way of challenging our thinking, and valuing the role that others can play in increasing our motivation and enjoyment in learning.

DRIVING WITH PEERS

We are helping each other to learn.

At the *driving* level, students are actively collaborating with each other in ways that intentionally drive learning forward and energize the motivation to want to progress. This is the most agentic form of engaging, meaning students have clear goals in mind, purposefully select strategies and a pathway for reaching that goal, and actively seek out others as valuable partners in learning. When working on their own, students actively reach out to others (including their peers) to discuss what they are learning, seek feedback on how to improve, get help in tackling challenges during learning, and come up with ideas for where to go next.

When *driving* in a social learning environment, students intentionally involve others in their learning. This includes sharing goals and plans for learning, collaborating with another person to tackle challenges, and seeking out help or feedback to guide improvement. However, optimizing peer engagement during learning involves more than just checking in or pairing up with peers at certain points in the learning process. Getting students *driving together* can take things to the next level and is essential if we want to harness the potential power of engaging with peers to learn.

LET'S GET **DRIVING TOGETHER!**

For *driving together* to be possible, students must want to unite in their efforts to learn and have a belief that together they can tackle the challenges of learning successfully. Students must invest their motivational resources into *driving* both their own learning and the progress of the group forward. As we learned in Chapter 4, motivation alone is not sufficient for *driving*. Students also need the right skills and the right kind of learning activity to empower *driving together*.

WHAT SKILLS DO STUDENTS NEED TO GET DRIVING TOGETHER?

Students who are *driving together* when learning in pairs or groups are demonstrating the same kind of behaviors associated with the *driving* pathway but also other important skills related to working with others successfully. This includes communicating ideas and sharing information, negotiating and resolving conflict, working together to set goals and make plans, and sharing the responsibility for evaluating both individual contributions and those of the group. In addition to these individual skills, highly engaged groups demonstrate certain characteristics, such as high levels of social sensitivity (see the following discussion), taking turns, having a sense of collective responsibility for the group's success, giving supportive feedback to each other, and treating each other as valued equals.

The authors of *Collective Student Efficacy* (Hattie et al., 2021) distinguish between the skills that individual students need ("I" skills) and those that the group needs ("we" skills) to develop high levels of collective efficacy and optimize learning during group activities. They describe the following key skills:

"I" Skills

- Having just the right level of self-confidence in their ability to contribute to the group. Too much confidence, and students might be resistant to the ideas of others because they believe they know best; too little, and students might doubt their ability to achieve success even when there is support available.
- Having a willingness to learn, embrace challenges, and learn from their mistakes.
- Being able to work with others to set group goals, follow directions, plan, make decisions, and delegate tasks.
- Contributing to the group's success by identifying challenges, finding strategies to overcome obstacles, sharing information, and staying on task.
- Having the verbal and nonverbal communication skills needed to share ideas, actively listen to others, negotiate, and engage in desirable argumentation.

"We" Skills

- Having high levels of social sensitivity (empathy, accepting others, acknowledging mistakes, being attuned to the moods and feelings of others, etc.).
- Believing "we will succeed" as a group.
- Having the motivation and determination to succeed together.
- Taking turns and taking on different roles within the group.
- Having a sense of collective responsibility for the group's success.

- Having a sense of responsibility for each other as equals in the group.
- Being able to give supportive feedback to each other without diminishing self-efficacy.

Importantly, just because a student has demonstrated the ability to take on the *driving* pathway successfully in individual learning situations does not mean the student is equipped with the necessary skills for working in a group. Likewise, *driving together* is not simply individual students *driving* while working on a group task. To prepare students for the challenge of *driving together*, we need to discuss the "I" and "we" skills involved in this pathway of engagement. If students have not yet developed these essential skills, we need to teach them.

DRIVING TOGETHER BY DESIGN

When we want students to reach the level of *driving together*, we need to think carefully about the type of task we design. Simply putting students in groups or pairs to work on an activity is not enough to support *driving together*. They need to be doing more than "doing" together; they need to be proactively collaborating to drive the group forward. In particular, we need to consider the level of challenge, how open the task is, the level of interdependence between students, and the nature of the groups.

LEVEL OF CHALLENGE

As we saw in the previous chapter, tasks that are too easy, too hard, or too boring are unlikely to inspire students to want to engage at the level of *driving together*. Tasks need to be challenging but achievable.

LEVEL OF OPENNESS

Open tasks that have a clear end goal but where the path to that goal is not obvious and/or there are multiple ways of reaching that goal are more conducive to *driving together* than closed tasks. Ideally, we are looking for a task that requires or invites different interpretations and ideas rather than a task where there is only a right way and a wrong way.

LEVEL OF INTERDEPENDENCE

When tasks require students to interact, coordinate their efforts, communicate, and cooperate, this is more conducive to engaging as a group (e.g., jigsaw). In contrast, tasks that make it easier for students to work on their own or leave it to others to do the work are less likely to support *driving together*.

GROUP SIZE

When planning, pay attention to the size of your groups. More does not mean better and can increase the chances of some students deciding to sit back and let others do the work, of social conflicts occurring within the group, and of challenges being involved in coordinating the contributions and motivation within the larger group. Larger groups are possible when there are structures in place that clarify what individual students are responsible for and what role they play.

EMPOWERING STUDENTS FOR *DRIVING TOGETHER*

When it comes to *driving together*, students need to know what it will look like when done successfully. In previous chapters, we looked at the different pathways of engaging and disengaging from learning and how students might use the behaviors described to set intentions, monitor engagement, and identify the next steps for engagement and learning. To help students accomplish this while *driving together*, we need to expand the *driving* pathway to include both the "I" and "we" skills needed for *driving together*. These behaviors aim to clarify for students the success criteria for being a highly engaged learner in a highly engaged group. The following are some of the general behaviors you might see individuals and groups demonstrating when *driving together*. Ideally, you will work with your students to co-construct "I" and "we" behaviors that are relevant to the learning activity and use language that your students understand.

DRIVING TOGETHER PATHWAY	
"I" SKILLS	**"WE" SKILLS**
I share my ideas with the group.	We accept and value each other.
I listen to the ideas of others.	We acknowledge our mistakes.
I work with others to set goals, make plans, and delegate tasks.	We listen and try to understand each other.
I evaluate what I have done and look for ways to improve.	We look out for each other's feelings.
I ask others for feedback.	We solve problems together.
I identify obstacles and share my ideas for overcoming these.	We take turns and take on different roles.
I challenge others in a respectful and supportive way.	We give each other supportive feedback.
	We share the responsibility for our group's success.

VALUING AND EVALUATING
DRIVING TOGETHER

To improve the quality of engagement within groups and the impact of group learning activities on student learning, we need to evaluate both individual students' engagement within the group and the group's engagement in the learning activity. Individual students need to know how they are doing and how they can improve their skills in *driving together*, and the "I" skills provide a useful reference point for this during the checking-in process. Students can be prompted to reflect on their engagement in the group using evidence to support their evaluation, including evidence that comes from other group members—for example, by asking a partner for feedback on their communication skills. Each student is encouraged and supported to identify a goal for improving the "I" skills in *driving together*.

Groups can also be prompted to use the "we" skills to check in on the engagement of the group. What evidence do students have that the group is highly engaged and *driving together*? What is something the group might need to work on? Groups work together to identify their goal for improving their "we" skills in *driving together*.

Finally, it is useful to consider how you will assess learning when group or pair work is involved. How might you evaluate individuals' contributions and the group's work? How might you provide feedback to both individuals and the group? Importantly, when making these decisions, we want to show that we stand by our claims that successful *driving together* requires the active engagement of each individual and the group as a whole.

TACKLING DISENGAGEMENT

As students become more engaged in learning, peers become an important resource for energizing motivation and collaborating to take learning forward. But what happens when students choose to disengage from learning? What does this mean for their peers? When it comes to disengaging, the impact on peers can range from negligible (e.g., if a student chooses to *withdraw* during an activity where individuals are working alone) to significant (e.g., if a student chooses to actively *disrupt* the learning of peers).

WITHDRAWING AND PEERS

This passive form of disengagement is similar to *participating* in that any interaction with peers is likely to be directed by the teacher. For example, it could be a directive to sit in a group or work with a partner during an activity, in which case the student might sit with peers while *withdrawing* from the activity. When a teacher comes by, the student may pretend to be working on the task and then stop once the teacher goes away. This is commonly referred to as "social loafing," and occurs when the student sits back and lets others within the group complete the work. Social loafing is an example of *withdrawing*.

In a group situation, having one or more persons choose to *withdraw* their effort and input can have a negative influence on the group outcomes, cause frustration and conflict within the group, and influence others to choose a path of disengaging as they lose confidence in the ability of the group to succeed or motivation to invest the effort needed to pick up the slack. When other students in the group also choose to engage in social loafing, this can escalate the level of disengagement if those students decide to engage in off-task behaviors like talking together (Linnenbrink-Garcia et al., 2011). Even though this passive form of disengaging might seem less serious, the potential impact on the learning and engagement of others is concerning. As we saw in Chapter 5, this is even more so because of the less visible nature of this form of disengaging.

AVOIDING AND PEERS

When students choose to *avoid*, they choose to engage in other things to avoid the learning activity or task in front of them. If the students are meant to be working by themselves, their behaviors may or may not affect others. For example, finding an excuse to leave the room might present little disruption to others, but choosing to move around the room or talk to another student might distract others trying to engage. Sometimes, students can choose to become partners in *avoiding* by doing things like talking together or playing with materials together. In a group situation, students who choose to engage in *avoiding* behaviors can have similar effects to *withdrawing* because they are choosing not to contribute to the group's progress, but may also cause a distraction to others in their group (and even groups nearby), which further compromises the potential for the group to fully engage and learn together.

DISRUPTING AND PEERS

At this level, students who are *disrupting* have chosen a path that aims to influence the engagement and learning of their peers. They are actively trying to disrupt and distract others from learning. This may include trying to disrupt other students (e.g., trying to engage them in an argument), trying to disrupt the group of students they are meant to be working with (e.g., bullying others, making fun of others, or trying to make others feel uncomfortable), or trying to disrupt the whole class (e.g., causing a major disturbance by engaging in high-level aggressive behavior). Students who choose this pathway of disengaging can have a significant negative impact on the engagement and learning of their peers.

THE INFLUENCE OF PEERS ON MOTIVATION AND ENGAGEMENT

Now that we have a better understanding of how students engage with each other at different levels of engagement, it is time to look at what the research has to say about the influence of peers on motivation and engagement.

THE INFLUENCE OF PEERS ON MOTIVATION

Peers have the potential to energize students' inner motivational resources by supporting their needs for autonomy, competence, and relatedness (Furrer et al., 2014). When peers show warmth and respect to each other, talk and listen to each other, provide emotional support to each other, and share in each other's experiences of learning, this contributes to their feelings of *relatedness* and connection to others in the classroom community. When students give and receive feedback from each other, create shared goals for learning, successfully resolve conflicts that arise during learning, provide each other with models of successful learning, and provide support to each other during learning, this contributes to a feeling of *competence* and confidence in their ability to take on the challenge of learning successfully. Finally, peers can support each other's need for *autonomy* when they try to understand each other's views, share ideas, explain the relevance of a learning activity to each other, and negotiate with each other to find a mutually acceptable solution or path forward.

The effect of peers can be either positive or negative depending on the level of engagement of those peers and the level of involvement with the teacher. In one study, students who felt supported by both their peers and the teacher reported the highest levels of engagement, while students who associated with disengaged peers and felt their teacher did not care about them reported the biggest declines in engagement over time (Vollet et al., 2017). The same study also found that when students belonged to a peer group of engaged students, this provided some protection against the negative impact of having a teacher who provided low levels of support or care, and when students perceived high levels of teacher support, this provided some protection from the negative effect of associating with disengaged peers.

Other studies have found that highly motivated students were more likely to be part of peer groups that were also more motivated, and less motivated students were more likely to be part of groups that were also less motivated (Sage & Kindermann, 1999). This can lead to a "rich get richer" effect where motivated peer groups maintain and energize their motivation but less motivated peer groups remain that way or become even less motivated over time. You may have some experience with this yourself, as one sixth-grade teacher did:

"I know in my experience I have definitely found that students who are less engaged are going to be friends with other students who are less engaged, and students who are highly engaged are going to be friends with students who are highly engaged. So in terms of peers, they probably play a big role because if I'm not engaged and I'm sitting next to my friend, I'm going to start talking to you and you're going to become less engaged because I'm not engaged. But, if I'm highly engaged and you're sitting there and you see that I'm highly engaged, you're going to have that motivation to go, 'Well, he's doing that, so I'm going to start doing that too.' I suppose that is my dilemma, trying to get that balance right, getting them next to people they feel comfortable with but also people who are going to be a good influence on each other."

PEERS AS PARTNERS IN ENGAGEMENT

We have an understanding of the different ways that students might engage (or disengage) with each other during learning and some evidence about the influence that peers can have on student engagement and motivation. But what about intentionally entering into a partnership with a peer to share the responsibility for each other's engagement? Having established the idea of a partnership between teacher and student, can we extend this idea and apply it to peers? If we teach the language and process of managing engagement, there is no reason why students cannot learn to apply these skills to peer partnerships. It is not sustainable for the teacher to be the only engagement partner for each individual student. If we are serious about supporting students to act with agency when it comes to learning and engagement, then we need to work with them to develop the necessary skills and knowledge to take the reins with this, just as they do when they are *driving* their learning. At the *driving* level, students use their peers as a valuable resource to help them progress toward their goals. In the same way, peers can become a valuable resource for managing engagement.

SETTING INTENTIONS FOR ENGAGEMENT

The peer partnership begins with sharing intentions for engagement. There is a certain level of useful accountability when students share their plans for engaging in learning rather than just keeping them to themselves, especially when they know they are going to have to check in with their partner later on. At the start, it might help to have a simple script or prompts for the students to refer to as they share. For example, the sharing of intentions might look something like this:

Partner 1: "I'm setting my intention at *investing* because . . ."

Partner 2: "Okay, what things from the *investing* pathway are you planning to do first?"

Partner 1: "I think I will start by . . ."

Partner 2: "Great! What will you do if you get stuck?"

Partner 1: "Maybe I can . . ."

Then the partners will swap and repeat the same process. To support students as they practice this step, you might do the following:

- Make sure that students have easy access to the list of behaviors on each engagement pathway to help them select their first steps.

- Help the class come up with a list of strategies for what to do when you get stuck. Keep adding to this list when students come up with new ideas that work in getting them back on track.

As students become more familiar and skilled with the process, you may find students come up with their own ways of sharing intentions and plans with each other.

CHECKING IN ON ENGAGEMENT

When it is time to check in on engagement, students will reconnect with their partners to see how things are going. As with sharing intentions, it will help to have clear guidelines for what is expected during the check-in. The essential elements of the check-in include an evaluation of actual engagement against the intentions for engagement, as well as evidence to support this evaluation. In simple terms, *how did you go*, and *how do you know?* It might look something like this if a student has achieved the intention:

> Partner 1: "You planned to be on the *investing* pathway. How did that go?"
>
> Partner 2: "I think I was at *investing*, but maybe a little *driving* too."
>
> Partner 1: "How do you know you were at *investing*? What did you do that makes you think you may have been *driving* a bit?"
>
> Partner 2: "If I look at the *investing* pathway, I was doing these five things. Then at the end, I asked the person I was working with for some feedback on the part that I had done because I wasn't sure how to improve it."

If the student has not achieved the intention, it might look like this:

> Partner 1: "You planned to be on the *investing* pathway. How did that go?"
>
> Partner 2: "I think maybe I got stuck in *participating* instead."
>
> Partner 1: "What makes you think you may have been *participating* instead of *investing*?"
>
> Partner 2: "If I look at the *investing* pathway, I did ask a couple of questions, but that is about all. I spent most of the time just listening to others and then focusing on getting the work done. So that is more *participating*, I think."

Students need to understand that their role is to help others reflect on what happened and explain their thinking using evidence. This is not about judgment; if students find they have been on a pathway of disengaging, the process is the same.

You can come up with a list of questions that can be used by students to support their partner's thinking—for example, "What makes you think that?" or "Can you give an example of how you . . . ?" or "What things did you do that are on that pathway?"

Give students plenty of practice to develop their skills in checking in and helping someone else to check in. Be on the lookout for great examples of students using evidence to evaluate their engagement, and great examples of students helping each other to think hard about their engagement.

WHERE TO NEXT FOR ENGAGEMENT?

When students have had a chance to evaluate their engagement, they are ready to plan what to do next. Partners help each other think about engagement and plan for engagement, but they don't do the thinking or planning for each other. Students are not responsible for their partner's engagement, and they are there not to solve each other's engagement problems, only to help each other find their own solutions. The focus of this step is on setting a new goal and making a plan for engagement, as well as identifying any help needed to achieve that goal. Three questions guide partner discussions during this step:

What is your goal for engagement now?

How will you get there?

Do you need any help?

Depending on whether the check-in is at the end of a learning experience or in the middle of it, the goal might be specific to an activity or task (e.g., stay on the *investing* pathway), or it might be a more general goal about furthering student engagement (e.g., doing more *driving*). To help students during this step, consider doing the following:

- Co-construct some goals for engagement to demonstrate what that might look like. Try to include a goal for moving to a higher level of engagement, a goal for maintaining the same level of engagement, and a goal for moving from a pathway of disengaging to a pathway of engaging.

- Discuss the difference between having an intention or goal for a specific activity and having a bigger goal for where you want to get to with your engagement. For example, our intentions for specific activities might fluctuate between *participating* and *driving* depending on what is involved, while our goals for engagement are focused on mastering the skills needed to manage engagement challenges and take on the responsibilities of *driving*.

- Discuss different situations where students might need help reaching their engagement goal, and come up with ideas for how to get that help. Refer students to this discussion to help them reflect on any help they might need while they plan.

BECOMING EFFECTIVE
ENGAGEMENT PARTNERS

Once students have been introduced to the language of engagement (the forms and pathways) and the process for engagement (setting intentions, checking in, and deciding where to go next), you can begin to prepare them for the peer partnership. The key is to be very clear about what to do and how to do it, then provide plenty of opportunities to practice and develop their skills. To help them to become effective engagement partners for their peers, you could do the following:

- **Model the process for students** so they can see it in action. You could do this with another adult or work with a student as your partner while the rest of the class watches on. When modeling, explain each part of the process as you go. If you want the students to use resources (e.g., a list of behaviors for different engagement pathways), model how they would do this.

- **Demonstrate good examples and not-so-good examples** to give students an understanding of what success looks like. Ask them to provide feedback and suggestions on how to improve when you demonstrate the not-so-good example.

- **Demonstrate different kinds of situations** to prepare students for the range of partnership experiences they might find themselves in. For example, demonstrate what it looks like when both partners are highly engaged and everything is going well, but also what it looks like when someone is disengaged and things are not going so well. Agree on when students might need to call on other students or the teacher to help them.

- **Create success criteria for the partnership** to clarify what the partners need to do to be successful. These can be phrased as "we" criteria to emphasize the dual responsibility of the partnership.

- **Create success criteria for individuals** to clarify what each student needs to do to engage in the different steps in the process successfully. These can be phrased as "I" criteria to emphasize the personal responsibility of the individual students for their own engagement and to their engagement partners.

- **Provide opportunities for students to partner with different peers**. Rather than always working with the same partner, get students to work with a range of different peers as partners—for example, by randomly assigning partners (e.g., using named sticks pulled from a jar) to keep it fair—rather than trying to pair students intentionally based on achievement levels or friendships. This provides students with greater opportunities to learn from each other and helps develop mutual respect within the group (Hattie et al., 2021).

- **Ask them to reflect on the process and give feedback** on how it's working. If needed, work together to make improvements.

- **Provide feedback to students** on their skills in using the process to manage engagement and their skills in partnering with a peer for engagement.

Now that the partnership is not just between the teacher and the student, it becomes a network of engagement partners sharing in the responsibility of engagement and learning within the group. In the next chapter, we will build on this idea to look at how we can cultivate a culture of engagement within our classroom. Before we do that, take a moment to set some intentions for how you will prepare your students for *driving together* and becoming effective engagement partners for each other.

TIME TO REFLECT

You started the chapter by reflecting on your previous experiences of peers influencing engagement. Now it is time to think ahead and make a plan for developing peer engagement within your classroom.

What initial goal do you have in mind for your class?

What will your first steps be?

What challenges do you anticipate, and how can you overcome these challenges?

How can you develop your own network of engagement partnerships with your peers?

CHAPTER 7

Cultivating a Culture of Engagement

"School culture can encourage or inhibit active students; it can make a student feel welcome or intimidated; and it can encourage or quash academic motivation. As teachers, we have the opportunity to foster positive changes to the everyday experience in our schools. Investing time in improving school culture is worth the effort."

—Brad Kuntz (2012, p. 8)

Reimagining student engagement is not a "to-do list" of activities that will instantly transform student engagement in your classroom. Instead, it requires work and time to change the way we think about engagement in learning. Both students and teachers need time to learn the new language, understand the new rules and expectations, and develop the skills they will need for their role in the engagement process. This final chapter will look at the culture we want to develop in our classroom to optimize everyone's— teachers' and students'—engagement in learning.

A CULTURE OF ENGAGEMENT

We often hear about the importance of classroom culture for student outcomes like well-being and achievement. A recent synthesis of research studies reported that classroom climate is positively associated with motivation, engagement, academic achievement, and social competence (Wang et al., 2020). The culture of a classroom is characterized by the instructional practices used, the interactions and relationships between people, and the organization and management of the classroom. From this perspective, classroom culture represents *the way we do things in this class*. It gives us an insight into what is expected of different people in the classroom, the processes and patterns of teaching and learning, and the norms for behaving and interacting within that environment. In this sense, classroom culture is a product of things that have been done previously, an outcome of what has happened in that classroom up until this point. It is less clear whether the culture is the result of a planned process to get to that point, or whether engagement is an explicit focus within that environment or more of an implicit understanding. How can we cultivate a culture that optimizes engagement?

culture (n)

From the Latin *cultura*, meaning "to cultivate," the act or process of tilling the land in preparation for growth.

1800s: The sense of collective customs, beliefs, habits, and material objects that constitute a people's way of life.

If we take a broader view of the meaning of *culture*, we see that it refers to both the process of preparing for something to grow and the products or achievements of the people who are involved. Culture involves a collaboration that is focused on growth and development. If our goal is to have a classroom culture that optimizes engagement, then we need to consider the process of preparing for that goal as well as the success criteria that will tell us when we have achieved that goal. How do we prepare for the growth of our engagement partnership? What do we hope to achieve as partners in engagement?

TILLING THE LAND—PREPARING TO GROW THE ENGAGEMENT PARTNERSHIP

As we have discussed throughout this book, the idea of collaborating with students to improve engagement in learning represents a departure from the more traditional battle over engagement. It involves many changes for both students and teachers, including changes to the language that we use for engagement, changes to the roles and responsibilities for engagement, and changes to the expectations for engagement. It also involves new processes and ways of doing things. Change can be hard, and we must invest time and effort into preparing everyone for the partnership. Although it can take time to see and feel the results of our efforts, you will likely notice some impact along the way. Several teachers have described the positive impact of taking the simple step of presenting and discussing the different forms of engagement and disengagement from the continuum. Be on the lookout for signs that your engagement partnerships are beginning to grow with each step you take. There is nothing like success to energize your motivation to keep going.

As we prepare for growing engagement, three anchor points can guide us: the inner motivational resources that drive learning, the partners and processes that will support engagement, and the language that we use to think about and discuss engagement.

LEARNING THE LANGUAGE OF ENGAGEMENT

One of the first things that we can do to prepare for the engagement partnership is to develop a shared language for engagement. That is, we need to learn how to "talk the talk" of engagement and learning. This includes expanding the vocabulary that we have for engagement, learning the language of inner motivation, defining what it means to be a successfully engaged learner, and redefining failure and disengagement. We do this with our students, seeking their input and insights, as a way of building their autonomy and helping them to take ownership over the language we use as we become partners in engagement.

Throughout the book, we have looked at different ways of introducing the language from the continuum (i.e., the different forms of engagement and the behaviors associated with them) and inviting students to share their perspectives on these. For example, in Chapter 5 we looked at a *Looks like/Feels like/Sounds like* thinking routine to facilitate a discussion on *withdrawing*. Recording the group's thinking and having this on display can provide a useful reference point during lessons to support students as they set intentions for engagement and evaluate their engagement during the check-in process. You might come up with other ways of creating visible resources for you and your students to use, such as asking them to create visual representations of each form of engagement and disengagement including words and images. Be open to adding more things or making adjustments to these resources as a way of tracking changes in the group's thinking or understanding.

Along with the language of engagement, we also need to develop a common understanding and vocabulary for discussing inner motivation as the essential fuel for our engagement in learning. Once again, we do this with students and put this into a language and context that is meaningful for them. Providing students with a specific reference point will allow you to explore the idea that our inner motivational resources can fluctuate depending on the context for learning. This could be a subject or class (e.g., English) or an activity (e.g., writing). It might also help to describe these as "I" statements given their internal nature. For example: *In this class, I feel like I am a good learner.* To help students understand how these inner feelings can either fill up our motivational tank or leave it feeling empty, we can describe both motivating and demotivating feelings. For example: *In this class, I find the things we do really interesting/I feel bored and have no interest in learning.* Try to come up with a couple of statements that represent both the positive and negative sides of each source of inner motivation (autonomy, competence, relatedness, interest, value); you can always add more as you go. Later, we will look at how these statements can be used to collect evidence of student motivation.

Finally, given learning is the goal of our engagement, we need to make sure that everyone has a clear understanding of what we mean by *learning*. This might involve redefining what it means to be a successful student if the current culture is focused on compliance, performance, or end product (getting it right, getting it done, doing it quickly) rather than learning as a process (making progress, improving, mastering). We might also need to change the way we talk about challenges, mistakes, and failures. If students have developed a belief that making mistakes is bad, rather than an opportunity to learn, they will be less willing to take on the challenges that will accelerate their learning. Our engagement partnership relies on a language of learning that places a high value on challenge, persistence, improvement, and collaboration.

TAKING IT INTO THE CLASSROOM

Before you start to develop the language of engagement in your classroom, it is a good idea to find out what the current language is. How do you and your students think about and talk about learning and engagement? This will give you a good starting point to refer to as you plan, and a useful reference point for tracking changes to the way the group uses the language you are trying to develop.

Start by reflecting on your understanding and beliefs about engagement and learning using the same questions you will use with your students.

Ask your students what they think about learning, and make a record of their responses. The idea is to find out what they have in mind when they think about successfully engaging in learning. You can use the following questions or come up with your own:

What do good learners do?

How do you know when you have been successful in learning?

Why do you learn?

How do the students' responses compare with your own? Are there beliefs about learning that will be useful for engagement (e.g., a belief that learning takes effort)? Are there beliefs that might prevent students from getting actively engaged (e.g., a belief that good learners never make mistakes)? How can you address these beliefs as you prepare the students for taking on the responsibility of *driving*?

PREPARING TO ENERGIZE INNER MOTIVATION

Once students have an understanding of what we mean by *inner motivation*, we can use the language of inner motivation to dig a bit deeper into how these inner resources act as fuel for our engagement. This includes developing a greater awareness of our motivation and the things that motivate us to want to learn, and the things that demotivate us and make us want to disengage from learning. We also want to learn strategies that can help us to fill up our tank of motivation.

Developing an Awareness of Motivation

It is difficult for teachers to monitor student motivation due to its internal nature (Lee & Reeve, 2012). For this reason, we will need our engagement partners to provide us with feedback on their inner motivation. It may take time for students to develop an awareness of their feelings of being motivated and demotivated and the language to be able to communicate this to others. We can help by giving them frequent opportunities to reflect on their motivation and talk about it using the language we are learning. This will have limited value if they are not also offered a variety of different learning experiences and strategies to reflect on. This variety will provide a better foundation for students to build their understanding of what motivates them and what demotivates them, and what strategies can help them move from demotivated to motivated. If we always do things the same way, students' capacity to learn how to regulate motivation and take actions to energize motivation will be limited.

TAKING IT INTO THE CLASSROOM

Give students practice by stopping at different times during learning and during different kinds of activities (e.g., while they are working by themselves, at the end of an activity, while working on a group activity, during a period of teacher-led instruction) and having them rate their motivation levels. You could create a simple rating scale from 1 (*I don't want to do this*) to 5 (*Please don't stop me; I want to keep going*). They can use their fingers to quickly indicate their motivation level at that moment. Ask for a few volunteers from both the motivated (4 and 5) and demotivated (1 and 2) groups to share the feelings they are having. If any students are sitting on the fence at a level 3, ask them to explain their feelings.

Alternatively, you could use a visual reference point like the *Motivation Tank* (Figure 7.1) to help students reflect on their motivation levels. Adapt it to fit your context and needs, and use it to check in on student motivation levels during a lesson, or to track changes to motivation over time and across different situations.

Encourage students to connect their motivation to their ability to engage. You can do this in an autonomy-supportive way by using language such as the following: *It sounds like you are feeling frustrated because this is the same thing we do every week. Do you think doing it in a more interesting way would help you want to engage?* This approach can also support them to start looking for solutions to their motivational challenges. Having lots of opportunities to practice this will help students to become more aware of their patterns of motivation—for example, *I've noticed that I am often demotivated during whole-group discussions but more motivated when I get to work on investigations with a few other people.* Acknowledge these insights as very important discoveries that will help the students to solve the problem of how to fill up their motivational tank so that they can get *driving.*

FIGURE 7.1 The Motivation Tank

IN THIS CLASS I FEEL LIKE . . .

I am forced to do things I don't want to do

I am a failure when I make a mistake

I am excluded or treated unfairly

I am bored and have no interest in things

I can't see any point in learning

MOTIVATION TANK

EMPTY

FULL

I am free to make choices during learning

I can take on challenges and succeed

I trust the people I work with

I am really interested in the things we are learning

I want to learn because it is important to me

PREPARING FOR THE PROCESSES
THAT WILL SUPPORT ENGAGEMENT

In Chapter 3, we learned about the process of setting intentions for engagement, checking in on engagement, and planning the next steps for engagement. As with any new process, we need to teach the different steps and give students time to practice those steps. If your students are already familiar with setting intentions for learning and using success criteria to monitor their progress, then this will build on these existing practices. If these things are not familiar to you or your students, it might take a little more time to develop everyone's skills in setting goals for learning and engagement, describing the different pathways and steps toward that goal, and using those to monitor progress along the way.

This will be a case of learning by doing. Through the experience of going through the process and reflecting on it, students and teachers will not only get better at it, but they will also develop a deeper understanding of any patterns of engagement and the challenges they face with engagement. Be on the lookout for interesting insights, discoveries, and puzzling questions that the group can learn from and investigate. This might include students' sudden realization that they keep setting an intention for *driving* but end up on the *participating* pathway instead, providing a perfect opportunity to investigate why this is happening and what can be done to help them get more actively engaged. Or, you might make your own discovery about the types of activities that are most effective for getting students to *driving* and which ones are sending them on a pathway of disengaging. Growing our engagement partnership means sharing our discoveries and our questions, helping us to learn from and with each other.

TAKING IT INTO THE CLASSROOM

Try connecting students' reflections on their inner motivation to their reflections on their level of engagement. What do they notice? What connections do they make? Can they see a relationship between their motivation and their engagement? What things are puzzling? Look for opportunities to investigate questions that students have about motivation and engagement.

Use a provocation or thought-provoking question to encourage students to take their thinking even deeper:

- When motivation is low, the person will always choose a pathway of disengaging. Agree or disagree?
- Can you be on the driving pathway and have low motivation? Explain your reasoning.
- Is it possible to be highly motivated to learn and also disengaged from a learning activity? Explain or give an example.

PREPARING TO BE A PARTNER IN ENGAGEMENT

The idea of becoming partners in engagement may be new to your students. As it involves mutual responsibility, agreed-upon goals, and expectations for both parties, it is important to be clear about what they are agreeing to. Without a shared understanding of what we are doing and why we are doing it, our culture of engagement might be on shaky ground.

TAKING IT INTO THE CLASSROOM

Try constructing an *engagement contract* with your students to outline the important things about your engagement partnership. This can include the following:

- **Your beliefs about engagement** (e.g., Everyone is capable of learning to drive their learning forward with the support of their engagement partners. The more actively engaged we are, the more we will learn.)
- **The roles of students and teachers** (e.g., Students agree to share the responsibility for engagement, actively participate in the process, look for solutions to engagement challenges, and so on. Teachers agree to try and see things from the student's perspective, make sure that learning experiences are designed to be as engaging as possible, seek feedback from students and use this to improve, and manage disruptions in the classroom that make it hard to engage.)
- **The responsibilities of engagement partners** (e.g., We hold each other accountable for engagement. We ask each other for help when we need it. We give help and support when someone asks for it. We give each other feedback on engagement. We check in with each other on engagement. We work together to solve engagement challenges. We celebrate engagement successes.)

Invite everyone to contribute their ideas about what should go into the contract, then work with them to create a set of clear and concise

(Continued)

(Continued)

statements to reflect those discussions. Think about how you will display this contract for easy reference, and how you might get everyone to agree to it officially. For example, you could display it on a bulletin board and get everyone to sign it or put their handprint on it.

When we have this clear understanding of what engagement partners are responsible for, we can think about extending our partnerships beyond teacher–student and student–student. We may decide to partner with parents and discuss the role they can play in supporting student engagement. At times, we may reach out to colleagues or school counselors for support with engagement challenges, and they can become engagement partners as well. Identifying a network of potential engagement partners for yourself ahead of time will help you to prepare for the path ahead. Whom will you partner with to help you engage in learning about engagement?

REAPING THE REWARDS OF A CULTURE OF ENGAGEMENT

In Chapter 2, we looked at the idea of *signature pedagogies* associated with teaching in different professions (Shulman, 2005). These pedagogies are aimed at teaching students how to "think like a doctor" or "think like a lawyer," not just teaching them about the skills and knowledge that are needed in medicine or law. Throughout this book, we have looked at ways that students can learn to "think like a learner" and develop habits that empower them to regulate their motivation to learn, and take actions that will enable them to become actively engaged and successful learners. Now that we are reaching the end of the book, it's time to think ahead about what it might look like when our culture of engagement is established and has reached the stage where everyone has developed a habit of "thinking like a learner" and "being an engagement partner." If you were to set an intention or a goal for where you would like you and your students to get to, what would it be?

TIME TO REFLECT

As you embark on the journey of reimagining student engagement in your classroom, take a moment to think about what success might look like for you and your students. The following prompts might help you to describe your vision for engagement in your classroom:

If outsiders observed your class, what would they see? What would they hear?

From the student perspective, what would students be doing and thinking? What would they be feeling?

As the teacher, what would you be doing and thinking? What would you be feeling?

PLANNING A PATHWAY TO SUCCESS

Now that you have a vision in mind of where you want to get to, it's time to think about the pathway that might get you to that longer-term goal. A good first step is to take stock of where you are right now. What is the culture of engagement in your classroom now?

> *What is the language of learning and engagement currently?*
>
> *What do you know about the motivation of your students?*
>
> *What do students know about motivation and engagement?*
>
> *What processes and patterns are in place to support engagement?*
>
> *Who is responsible for engagement?*

You may have already started to investigate these questions while reading this book. If not, think about how you can gather information to help you take stock of where you are now. How can you involve the students and get their input? How can you involve other potential engagement partners (e.g., colleagues) to help you collect this information? Developing a rich picture of where you are starting from will help you to notice the signs of change when they occur. Collecting the same information at different points in time will also help you track that progress and development over time. Involve students in this process of monitoring the group's progress, and celebrate the successes along the way. Get everyone to be on the lookout for signs that people are "thinking like a learner" and "being an engagement partner."

The ideas presented in the previous section might give you some thoughts about where to start, and you might find that you can gather information about what students know and think as part of the process of introducing them to things like the engagement continuum and the concept of inner motivational resources.

What steps will you take first? As you start to plan the next steps for you and your students, think about what evidence you can collect along the way. How will you know if what you are doing is working? What impact are your actions having? Who are they impacting, and how? How can you involve the partners in this process?

A CULTURE OF ENGAGEMENT

As we saw earlier, *culture* has been described as the "collective customs and achievements of a people." It takes time and collective effort to develop before we get to the stage of being able to say, "This is us, and this is what we do." If we imagine a culture of engagement, we can imagine what the people in that culture might say:

> We have a **common language** for engagement, and we all know what we mean when we use the language of engagement.

> We agree on **the rules of engagement** and hold each other accountable for meeting the expectations for engagement.

> We **share the responsibility** for engagement, and we value and support each other as partners in engagement.

> We **make a habit** of checking in on engagement, which includes checking in with ourselves and checking in with others.

> **We value** learning, thinking, and taking on challenges that help us improve.

> **We value** the inner motivational resources that give us the fuel for engagement, and we support each other to energize those resources.

As you and your students develop your own culture of engagement, you might come up with your own statements to communicate your customs, values, habits, and achievements.

Undoubtedly, there will be challenges ahead and times when the motivation to persist will be tested. Don't give up. Reach out to your engagement partners—that is why they are there. Take time to celebrate the achievements along the way as evidence that you are making a difference in the way your students experience school and think about learning.

References

INTRODUCTION

Labaree, D. F. (2021). The dynamic tension at the core of the grammar of schooling. *Phi Delta Kappan, 103*(2), 28–32.

Mehta, J., & Datnow, A. (2020). Changing the grammar of schooling: An appraisal and a research agenda. *American Journal of Education, 126*(4), 491–498.

Tyack, D., & Tobin, W. (1994). The "grammar" of schooling: Why has it been so hard to change? *American Educational Research Journal, 31*(3), 453–479.

CHAPTER 1

Angus, M., McDonald, T., Ormond, C., Rybarczyk, R., Taylor, A., & Winterton, A. (2009). *The pipeline project: Trajectories of classroom behaviour and academic progress: A study of engagement with learning.* Edith Cowan University. http://www.bass.edu.au/files/5413/9925/8294/Pipeline_Report_Dec_2009.pdf

Association for Supervision and Curriculum Development. (2016). *The engagement gap: Making each school and every classroom an all-engaging learning environment.* A report on the Spring 2016 ASCD Whole Child Symposium. https://files.ascd.org/staticfiles/ascd/pdf/siteASCD/wholechild/spring2016wcsreport.pdf

Berry, A. (2020). Disrupting to driving: Exploring upper primary teachers' perspectives on student engagement. *Teachers and Teaching, 26*(2), 145–165.

Conner, J. O., & Pope, D. C. (2013). Not just robo-students: Why full engagement matters and how schools can promote it. *Journal of Youth and Adolescence, 42*(9), 1426–1442.

Eccles, J. (2016). Engagement: Where to next? *Learning and Instruction, 43,* 71–75.

Fisher, D., Frey, N., & Hattie, J. (2020). *The distance learning playbook, Grades K–12: Teaching for engagement and impact in any setting.* Corwin.

Fredricks, J. A., Blumenfeld, P., & Paris, A. H. (2004). School engagement: Potential of the concept, state of the evidence. *Review of Educational Research, 74*(1), 59–109.

Fredricks, J. A., Reschly, A. L., & Christenson, S. L. (2019). Interventions for student engagement: Overview and state of the field. In J. A. Fredricks, A. L. Reschly, & S. L. Christenson (Eds.), *Handbook of student engagement interventions* (pp. 1–8). Academic Press.

Goss, P., Sonnemann, J., & Griffiths, K. (2017). *Engaging students: Creating classrooms that improve learning.* Grattan Institute.

Hodges, T. (2018, October 25). *School engagement is more than just talk.* Gallup Education. https://www.gallup.com/education/244022/school-engagement-talk.aspx

Janosz, M., Archambault, I., Morizot, J., & Pagani, L. S. (2008). School engagement trajectories and their differential predictive relations to dropout. *Journal of Social Issues, 64*(1), 21–40.

Jenkins, L. (n.d.). *Education's invisible problem.* LtoJ Consulting Group. https://ltojconsulting.com/educations-invisible-problem

Panadero, E. (2017). A review of self-regulated learning: Six models and four directions for research. *Frontiers in Psychology, 8,* 422.

Pope, D. C. (2001). *"Doing school": How we are creating a generation of stressed out, materialistic, and miseducated students.* Yale University Press.

Wang, M. T., & Peck, S. C. (2013). Adolescent educational success and mental health vary across school engagement profiles. *Developmental Psychology*, 49(7), 1266.

CHAPTER 2

Baraf, A. (2019). The Met High School: Engaging youth one student at a time. In J. A. Fredricks, A. L. Reschly, & S. L. Christenson (Eds.), *Handbook of student engagement interventions* (pp. 359–373). Academic Press.

Cheon, S. H., Reeve, J., & Vansteenkiste, M. (2020). When teachers learn how to provide classroom structure in an autonomy-supportive way: Benefits to teachers and their students. *Teaching and Teacher Education*, 90, 103004.

Deci, E. L., & Ryan, R. M. (2000). The "what" and "why" of goal pursuits: Human needs and the self-determination of behavior. *Psychological Inquiry*, 11(4), 227–268.

Kennedy, M. (2016). Parsing the practice of teaching. *Journal of Teacher Education*, 67(1), 6–17.

Klem, A. M., & Connell, J. P. (2004). Relationships matter: Linking teacher support to student engagement and achievement. *The Journal of School Health*, 74(7), 262–273.

Matos, L., Reeve, J., Herrera, D., & Claux, M. (2018). Students' agentic engagement predicts longitudinal increases in perceived autonomy-supportive teaching: The squeaky wheel gets the grease. *Journal of Experimental Education*, 86, 592–609.

Reeve, J. (2009). Why teachers adopt a controlling motivating style toward students and how they can become more autonomy supportive. *Educational Psychologist*, 44(3), 159–175.

Reeve, J. (2016). Autonomy-supportive teaching: What it is, how to do it. In W. C. Liu, J. C. K. Wang, & R. M. Ryan (Eds.), *Building autonomous learners* (pp. 129–152). Springer.

Reeve, J., Cheon, S. H., & Jang, H. (2020). How and why students make academic progress: Reconceptualizing the student engagement construct to increase its explanatory power. *Contemporary Educational Psychology*, 62, 101899.

Roorda, D. L., Koomen, H. M. Y., Spilt, J. L., & Oort, F. J. (2011). The influence of affective teacher-student relationships on students' school engagement and achievement: A meta-analytic approach. *Review of Educational Research*, 81(4), 493–529.

Sierens, E., Vansteenkiste, M., Goossens, L., Soenens, B., & Dochy, F. (2009). The synergistic relationship of perceived autonomy support and structure in the prediction of self-regulated learning. *British Journal of Educational Psychology*, 79(1), 57–68.

Staricoff, M. (2021). *The joy of not knowing: A philosophy of education transforming teaching, thinking, learning and leadership in schools*. Routledge.

CHAPTER 3

Black, P. J., & Wiliam, D. (2009). Developing the theory of formative assessment. *Educational Assessment, Evaluation and Accountability*, 21(1), 5–31.

Cauley, K. M., & McMillan, J. H. (2010). Formative assessment techniques to support student motivation and achievement. *The Clearing House: A Journal of Educational Strategies, Issues and Ideas*, 83(1), 1–6.

Coe, R. (2015, October 31). *What makes great teaching?* [Presentation]. IB World Regional Conference, Den Haag, Netherlands. https://www.ibo.org/globalassets/events/aem/conferences/2015/robert-coe.pdf

Corwin. (2021, October 19). *Doug Fisher & John Hattie: Collective student efficacy* [Video]. YouTube. https://youtu.be/BJPlVeylGmQ

Lee, W., & Reeve, J. (2012). Teachers' estimates of their students' motivation and engagement: Being in synch with students. *Educational Psychology*, 32(6), 727–747.

Shulman, L. (2005, February 6–8). *The signature pedagogies of the professions* of law, medicine, engineering, and the clergy: Potential lessons for the education of teachers [Presentation]. Math Science Partnerships (MSP) Workshop: "Teacher Education for Effective Teaching and Learning" Hosted by the National Research Council's Center for Education, Irvine, CA.

Skinner, E. A., & Pitzer, J. R. (2012). Developmental dynamics of student engagement, coping, and everyday resilience. In S. L. Christenson, A. L. Reschly, & C. Wylie (Eds.), *Handbook of research on student engagement* (pp. 21–44). Springer Science.

CHAPTER 4

Project Zero. (n.d.). *Project Zero's thinking routines toolbox.* Harvard Graduate School of Education. http://www.pz.harvard.edu/thinking-routines

Visible Learning Meta^x. (2021, August). *Global research database.* Corwin Visible Learning Plus. https://www.visible-learningmetax.com/influences

CHAPTER 5

Angus, M., McDonald, T., Ormond, C., Rybarczyk, R., Taylor, A. & Winterton, A. (2009). *The Pipeline Project: Trajectories of classroom behaviour and academic progress: A study of engagement with learning.* Edith Cowan University. http://www.bass.edu.au/files/5413/9925/8294/Pipeline_Report_Dec_ 2009.pdf

Assor, A. (2012). Allowing choice and nurturing an inner compass: Educational practices supporting students' need for autonomy. In S. Christenson, A. Reschly, & C. Wylie (Eds.), *Handbook of research on student engagement* (pp. 421–439). Springer Science.

Assor, A., Kalpan, H., Kanat-Maymon, Y., & Roth, G. (2005). Directly controlling teacher behaviors as predictors of poor motivation and engagement in girls and boys: The role of anger and anxiety. *Learning and Instruction, 15,* 397–413.

Earl, S. R., Taylor, I. M., Meijen, C., & Passfield, L. (2017). Autonomy and competence frustration in young adolescent classrooms: Different associations with active and passive disengagement. *Learning and Instruction, 49,* 32–40.

Fisher, D., & Frey, N. (2004). *Improving adolescent literacy: Strategies at work.* Pearson Prentice Hall.

Fredricks, J. A., Alfeld, C., & Eccles, J. (2010). Developing and fostering passion in academic and nonacademic domains. *Gifted Child Quarterly, 54,* 18–30.

Jang, H., Kim, E. J., & Reeve, J. (2016). Why students become more engaged or more disengaged during the semester: A self-determination theory dual-process model. *Learning and Instruction, 43,* 27–38.

Lamnina, M., & Chase, C. C. (2019). Developing a thirst for knowledge: How uncertainty in the classroom influences curiosity, affect, learning, and transfer. *Contemporary Educational Psychology, 59,* 101785.

Lee, W., & Reeve, J. (2012). Teachers' estimates of their students' motivation and engagement: Being in synch with students. *Educational Psychology, 32*(6), 727–747.

Nuthall, G. (2007). *The hidden lives of learners.* New Zealand Council for Educational Research Press.

Patall, E. A., Vasquez, A. C., Steingut, R. R., Trimble, S. S., & Pituch, K. A. (2016). Daily interest, engagement, and autonomy support in the high school science classroom. *Contemporary Educational Psychology, 46,* 180–194.

Paulsen, E., Bru, E., & Murberg, T. A. (2006). Passive students in junior high school: The associations with shyness, perceived competence and social support. *Social Psychology of Education, 9,* 67–81.

Pelletier, L. G., Séguin-Lévesque, C., & Legault, L. (2002). Pressure from above and pressure from below as determinants of teachers' motivation and teaching behaviors. *Journal of Educational Psychology, 94*(1), 186.

Reeve, J. (2009). Why teachers adopt a controlling motivating style toward students and how they can become more autonomy supportive. *Educational Psychologist, 44*(3), 159–175.

Reeve, J. (2016). Autonomy-supportive teaching: What it is, how to do it. In W. C. Liu, L. C. J. Wang, & R. M. Ryan (Eds.), *Building autonomous learners* (pp. 129–152). Springer, Singapore.

Reeve, J., & Cheon, S. H. (2016). Teachers become more autonomy supportive after they believe it is easy to do. *Psychology of Sport and Exercise, 22*, 178–189.

Skinner, E. A., & Belmont, M. J. (1993). Motivation in the classroom: Reciprocal effects of teacher behavior and student engagement across the school year. *Journal of Educational Psychology, 85*(4), 571.

Skinner, E., Furrer, C., Marchand, G., & Kindermann, T. (2008). Engagement and disaffection in the classroom: Part of a larger motivational dynamic? *Journal of Educational Psychology, 100*(4), 765–781.

Soenens, B., Sierens, E., Vansteenkiste, M., Dochy, F., & Goossens, L. (2012). Psychologically controlling teaching: Examining outcomes, antecedents, and mediators. *Journal of Educational Psychology, 104*, 108–120.

Stigler, J. W., & Hiebert, J. (2004). Improving mathematics teaching. *Educational Leadership, 61*(5), 12–17.

Strati, A. D., Schmidt, J. A., & Maier, K. S. (2017). Perceived challenge, teacher support, and teacher obstruction as predictors of student engagement. *Journal of Educational Psychology, 109*(1), 131–147.

Sullivan, A. M., Johnson, B., Owens, L. & Conway, R. (2014). Punish them or engage them? Teachers' views of unproductive student behaviors in the classroom. *Australian Journal of Teacher Education, 39*(6), 43–56.

Weybright, E. H., Schulenberg, J., & Caldwell, L. L. (2020). More bored today than yesterday? National trends in adolescent boredom from 2008 to 2017. *Journal of Adolescent Health, 66*(3), 360–365.

CHAPTER 6

Furrer, C., Skinner, E., & Pitzer, J. (2014). The influence of teacher and peer relationships on students' classroom engagement and everyday motivational resilience. *National Society for the Study of Education, 113*(1), 101–123.

Hattie, J., Fisher, D., Frey, N., & Clarke, S. (2021). *Collective student efficacy: Developing independent and inter-dependent learners.* Corwin.

Linnenbrink-Garcia, L., Rogat, T. K., & Koskey, K. L. K. (2011). Affect and engagement during small group instruction. *Contemporary Educational Psychology, 36*(1), 13–24.

Sage, N., & Kindermann, T. A. (1999). Peer networks, behavior contingencies, and children's engagement in the classroom. *Merrill-Palmer Quarterly, 45*(1), 143–171.

Vollet, J. W., Kindermann, T. A., & Skinner, E. A. (2017). In peer matters, teachers matter: Peer group influences on students' engagement depend on teacher involvement. *Journal of Educational Psychology, 109*(5), 635–665.

CHAPTER 7

Kuntz, B. (2012, September). ASCD community: Create a positive school culture. *Education Update, 54*(9), 8.

Lee, W., & Reeve, J. (2012). Teachers' estimates of their students' motivation and engagement: Being in synch with students. *Educational Psychology, 32*(6), 727–747.

Shulman, L. (2005, February 6–8). *The signature pedagogies of the professions of law, medicine, engineering, and the clergy: Potential lessons for the education of teachers* [Presentation]. Math Science Partnerships (MSP) Workshop: "Teacher Education for Effective Teaching and Learning" Hosted by the National Research Council's Center for Education, Irvine, CA.

Wang, M. T., Degol, J. L., Amemiya, J., Parr, A., & Guo, J. (2020). Classroom climate and children's academic and psychological wellbeing: A systematic review and meta-analysis. *Developmental Review, 57*, 100912.

Index

motivation and effort, 37, 53, 58, 62, 68, 99

motivation tank, 126, 128, 129

Negative feelings, 87, 100

Outcomes, 2, 11, 13, 43, 63, 124
 intended, 13–14

Partnership, 23, 33, 48, 55, 84, 97, 107–21, 124–25, 130, 133
 agentic, 3
 approach to disengagement, 79
 model, 24–25, 40
 in learning, 32, 94, 109
 peer, 116–17, 120
 with students, 120
Pathways of disengagement, 49, 52–53, 58, 115, 118–19, 129–30
 avoiding, 53, 72, 91–92, 114,
 disrupting, 53, 72, 86, 92–94, 114–115
 withdrawing, 52, 71, 72, 86, 89–91, 113–114
Pathways of engagement
 driving, 33, 48–49, 68–70, 72–75, 93–94, 108–113
 investing, 48–49, 58, 62–65, 67–69, 72–75, 107–108, 117–118
 participating, 47–49, 58, 59, 64–65, 66, 69, 72–75, 107, 118
Planned learning, 43
 activities, 10, 18–19, 31, 74, 107

experiences, 15–16, 18–19, 39, 44
Practice problems, 61, 100
Process, 70, 83, 125, 129
 checking-in, 52, 91, 113
 for setting intentions for engagement, 41, 129

Questions, asking, 16–17, 35, 47–48, 67, 73

Reeve, J., 28–30, 35, 40, 81, 82–83, 87, 100, 103, 127
Routines, 46, 67, 98
Rules of engagement, 21, 45–46, 54, 62, 65, 133

Shulman, L., 45–46, 131,
Soenens, B., 81–82
Success
 criteria, 41
 group, 110, 112

Taking action, 18, 36, 43, 46, 48, 54, 70
Teamwork, 105
Thinking, 17, 94, 96–97
 group's, 98, 125–26
 routines, 67, 91, 125

Visible Learning Meta^X, 36, 68

Wiliam, D., 41–42
Worksheets, 65, 100

Solutions YOU WANT | Experts YOU TRUST | Results YOU NEED

INSTITUTES

Corwin Institutes provide regional and virtual events where educators collaborate with peers and learn from industry experts. Prepare to be recharged and motivated!

corwin.com/institutes

ON-SITE PROFESSIONAL LEARNING

Corwin on-site PD is delivered through high-energy keynotes, practical workshops, and custom coaching services designed to support knowledge development and implementation.

www.corwin.com/pd

VIRTUAL PROFESSIONAL LEARNING

Our virtual PD combines live expert facilitation with the flexibility of anytime, anywhere professional learning. See the power of intentionally designed virtual PD.

www.corwin.com/virtualworkshops

CORWIN ONLINE

Online learning designed to engage, inform, challenge, and inspire. Our courses offer practical, classroom-focused instruction that will meet your continuing education needs and enhance your practice.

www.corwinonline.com

Visit **www.corwin.com**

PLSN209A8

A SAGE Publishing Company

Helping educators make the greatest impact

CORWIN HAS ONE MISSION: to enhance education through intentional professional learning.

We build long-term relationships with our authors, educators, clients, and associations who partner with us to develop and continuously improve the best evidence-based practices that establish and support lifelong learning.